Victorian and Edwardian Fashions from "La Mode Illustrée"

EDITED AND WITH AN
INTRODUCTION BY

JOANNE OLIAN

Curator Emeritus, Costume Collection
Museum of the City of New York

DOVER PUBLICATIONS, INC.
Mineola, New York

Copyright

Copyright © 1998 by Dover Publications, Inc.
All rights reserved under Pan American and International Copyright Conventions.

Bibliographical Note

Victorian and Edwardian Fashions from "La Mode Illustrée" is a new work, first published by Dover Publications, Inc., in 1998.

Library of Congress Cataloging-in-Publication Data

Victorian and Edwardian fashions from "La Mode Illustrée" / edited and with an introduction by JoAnne Olian.
     p.   cm.
  ISBN 0-486-29711-X (pbk.)
  1. Costume—France—History—19th century. 2. Costume—France—History—20th century. 3. Costume—Great Britain—History—19th century. 4. Costume—Great Britain—History—20th century. 5. Mode illustrée—History. I. Olian, JoAnne. II. La Mode illustreé.
GT871.V53   1998
391'.00944'09034—dc21   98-29316
                                                                          CIP

Manufactured in the United States of America
Dover Publications, Inc., 31 East 2nd Street, Mineola, N.Y. 11501

Book design by Carol Belanger Grafton

Introduction

Dress for women is the first of arts, the one that contains all the others.
It is her offensive armor, her harmonious palette.
OCTAVE UZANNE, *La Femme à Paris* (1894)

The symbiotic relationship between fashion and the arts has never been more apparent than in nineteenth-century France where dress was described in rhapsodic and minute detail by Balzac, Zola, Proust, Baudelaire, and Stephane Mallarmé who, in 1874, founded the short-lived magazine, *La Dernière Mode*, for which he covered fashion under the pseudonyms Marguerite de Ponty, Zizy, and Miss Satin. Baudelaire, exploring the relationship between women and dress, glorified woman thus: "[she is not] for the artist . . . merely the female of the human species. She is rather a goddess . . . the vast, iridescent clouds of draperies in which she envelops herself . . . are, so to speak, the attributes and the pedestal of divinity. . . . Show me the man who . . . has not enjoyed, in the most detached manner, the sight of a skillfully composed toilette, and has not carried away with him an image inseparable from the beauty of the woman wearing it, thus making the two, the woman and the dress, an indivisible whole." The paintings of his contemporaries Tissot, Beraud, et al were graphic testimony to Baudelaire's question, "What poet would dare, in painting the pleasure caused by the appearance of a beauty, to separate the woman from her costume?" Even Monet and Cezanne based canvases on engraved fashion plates from *La Mode Illustrée* and *Le Petit Courrier des Dames*.

The period of the Second Empire and the Belle Époque — slightly more than half a century beginning with the founding of *La Mode Illustrée* in 1860 and ending with the onset of World War I in 1914 — was a time of unprecedented change, characterized by a deluge of technological innovations that dramatically transformed daily life, from horse to iron horse to horseless carriage. Mass production methods enabled products to be turned out in quantities sufficient to supply a burgeoning consumer class. A new breed of merchant shrewdly concocted a climate of perpetual temptation, leading to the creation of new businesses catering to the insatiable, fast-changing desires of an affluent middle class. Before 1860, department stores were already established in New York and Paris selling "confections" (ready-made garments, consisting mostly of outerwear and undergarments at first), dress goods, and the astonishing assortment of accessories deemed vital to the sartorial well-being of the nineteenth-century customer. Only dresses were still made up individually by a dressmaker or the wearer herself. This traditional method of dressmaking was revolutionized by Charles Worth, the Englishman who founded the French haute couture industry. A man of his time, he was both artist and entrepreneur. He devised a system of standardized interchangeable components that allowed one pattern piece to be used for any number of designs and utilized the sewing machine for joining parts and sewing seams, reserving handwork for finishing and embroidery. Worth presented seasonal collections, showed them on live mannequins, signed his work with a label, and, by 1871, had over 1,200 workers in his employ.

The first illustration in this book was engraved after a photograph of the Empress Eugénie, one of a series by Disderi, a Paris photographer who conceived the *carte de visite* format in 1854 and was selling over 2,000 such postcards daily by 1862. By the date of the photograph, Worth would probably have been presented to the empress by Princess Pauline Metternich, the fashionable wife of the Austrian ambassador, and Eugénie might well be wearing one of his designs. The serendipitous confluence of the commanding Charles Worth and the compelling Eugénie set the sartorial tone for the glittering society of the Second Empire. Frederick Nietzsche may well have been thinking of the duo when he wrote, "Women believe in their dressmakers as in their god." In emulation of Louis XIV, who commanded his courtiers to wear a new costume for each appearance at Versailles as an impetus to the French fashion industry, Emperor Napoleon III let it be known that to wear a dress twice to the Palace of the Tuileries was to incur his utmost displeasure. For the fashion-loving court, especially the empress and the Princess Metternich, this could scarcely have been a hardship. According to Diana de Marly in *Worth, Father of Haute Couture* (1980), "it has been estimated that between Twelfth Night and Shrove Tuesday 1864 there were 130 balls in Paris," each necessitating suitable attire. The empress — young, beautiful, elegant, and possessing enormous style — set the tone for fashion during her reign. Even her coiffure, which provided a frame "like dove's wings along the sides of her delicious face," was seen everywhere. Dubbed Empress Crinoline, when she appeared at court in her voluminous-skirted Worths, Eugénie personified Théophile Gautier's description of the style, which he called a "pedestal for the upper torso," from which the "waist emerges elegant and slim, the upper body stands out advantageously, the entire person a gracious pyramid." The emperor used her as a walking endorsement for French textiles, providing a stimulus to the silk mills of Lyons, unparalleled since the time of Louis XIV. When Eugénie attended the opening of the Suez Canal in 1869 she is said to have taken 500 dresses, which she called her "political wardrobe." "Eugénie personified France as the world saw it then: as a country of inexhaustible energy and artistic vitality, a great power and the unquestioned center of cultured life. Eugénie and France, Eugénie and Paris, all seemed one and the same." (CIBA *Review*, no 46, May 1943.)

In 1870, the French defeat in the Franco-Prussian War brought an end to the reign of Napoleon III, but not to that of Charles Worth, who continued to dictate fashion so absolutely that the era was often called "The Age of Worth." Imperial patronage was replaced by an adoring clientele consisting of international society; "ladies well known on the banks of the Hudson and the Neva" (*Harper's Bazar*, October 19, 1872), who made semi-annual pilgrimages to the "pontiff of the skirt" at 7, rue de la Paix to be fitted for the requisite number of costumes for the coming season.

Beginning in 1860, the height of imperial splendor, while Worth was catering to the luxurious tastes of his far-flung nouveau riche clientele, another, practical, moderating influence began to be felt throughout France. It was that of Emmeline Raymond, whose philosophy of "economy in elegance," the antithesis of the unbridled extravagance and ostentation of the Second Empire, was promulgated by the magazine she founded, *La Mode Illustrée*.

While the doings of royalty were of consuming interest to middle-class readers, their own social functions required no less attention to dress than the most lavish ball at the Tuileries. The avid desire by a prospering bourgeoisie for information concerning fashion and manners accounts for the proliferation of periodicals devoted to those subjects between 1840 to 1875, when in France alone over sixty such magazines appeared. For Frenchwomen in the provinces as well as in Paris, *La Mode Illustrée*, subtitled *Journal de la Famil*, provided a touch of sophistication tempered by a large dose of housewifely practicality, a combination responsible in large measure for the magazine's popularity and its longevity (it flourished for more than three quarters of a century, until 1937). It was the first fashion periodical to publish weekly, in order to "avoid the inconveniences inherent in monthly journals, which cannot, where fashion is concerned, keep their readers au courant with all the latest trends, and find themselves, as regards their literary content, in the vexing alternative of shortening and mutilating their stories, in order to contain them in the space allotted, or to postpone for a month satisfying the curiosity aroused." Also the first to adopt a large format,

La Mode Illustrée was issued in four editions, the most deluxe of which contained a colored engraving every week. A three-month subscription was offered, but the serialized novels appearing regularly were an inducement to subscribe for a year, at 24 francs.

A forward-thinking woman who was to remain editor-in-chief of *La Mode Illustrée* until her death in 1902, Mme Raymond's avowed purpose was "to fulfill the cherished ambition of being useful." It was her hope that the magazine "would become indispensible," treasured by families as a "museum of memories," in which women could evoke the work that had "occupied their leisure," and the toilettes that had "adorned them." *La Mode Illustrée* did indeed have a niche in this society: home and domesticity were of paramount interest to women whose sole career was that of housewife—even the empress took "care of her own child as would an ordinary mother. She dresses him, rocks him, and sings him Spanish tunes."(Michelle Perrot, *History of Private Life, vol. 4*, 1990)

The magazine's fiftieth anniversary issue (November 21, 1909) paid homage to Mme Raymond, stating that, although she began publishing at "the height of political, economic and industrial prosperity of the Second Empire, when the new flowers that everyone wants to smell and gather, the flowers of progress, are blooming," she was "too prudent and sensible to believe in roses without thorns."

> An admirable feminine and maternal intuition makes her envisage and foresee all the effects of this revolution of mores and ideas penetrating, with the railroads, into the heart of the provinces and provincial women. She envisions the new exigences of this society which has discarded strict traditions, stripped of well-being, elegance and distraction; she is preoccupied with what mothers of families, women of the world, mistresses of households will have to face, many of whom, lacking in experience and discernment, risk living on the edge, or allowing themselves to be carried away beyond proper limits. She seeks a way to come to their aid, in this crisis . . . The means? it would be to create that which does not yet exist: a publication at once moral and practical, a sort of encyclopedia of woman comme il faut.

Since a nineteenth-century woman could be well-dressed only according to a strict code of correctness and appropriateness for the occasion, one's station in society, the season, and any number of additional constrictions, fashion and etiquette were inseparable.

> To bring her toilette into harmony, not only with herself, with her character, mood, age, face, complexion, and the color of her eyes and hair but also with her wealth and rank in society, with social events, hours of the day, and yearly seasonal changes, in other words with all the space she traversed, was the prime mystery of sartorial propriety . . . The diurnal and nocturnal time of aristocratic and high-bourgeois society was divided into pretexts, marked by a relentless tempo for dressing and undressing; and doing so appropriately involved a veritable gnosis. . . . [Etiquette books provided a] reference point of temporal and spatial oppositions (night/day, morning/evening, winter/summer, interior/exterior, town/country) that constituted basic dichotomies within which an impressive

armory of vestimentary opportunities could unfurl: the wardrobe. (Philippe Perrot, *Fashioning the Bourgeoisie*; translated by Richard Bienvenu, 1994.)

All this was by no means an exclusively French phenomenon. American women were equally preoccupied with etiquette and appropriate dress, occasioning countless American books and periodicals devoted to both subects. In *Women of New York* (1870), George Ellington exaggerated, "The elite do not wear the same dress twice. If you can tell us how many receptions she has in a year, how many weddings she attends, how many balls she participates in, how many dinners she gives, how many parties she goes to, how many operas and theatres she patronizes, we can approximate somewhat to the cost and size of her wardrobe. It is not unreasonable to suppose that she has two new dresses of some sort for every day in the year, or seven hundred and twenty. Now to purchase all these, to order them made and to put them on afterward consumes a vast amount of time. Indeed, the woman of society does little but doff and don dry goods."

Mrs. M. E. W. Sherwood's, *The American Code of Manners* and *Manners and Social Usages*, both published in 1884, were as ubiquitous as the Bible in some parlors. Sarah Josepha Hale, the editor of *Godey's Lady's Book* from 1828 to 1878, was cut from the same cloth as Emmeline Raymond, sharing her determination to educate the housewife regarding her duties, provide her with sentimental fiction and genteel needlework, and keep her abreast of the latest fashions. *Godey's* addressed itself to women beyond the cities, while *Harper's Bazar*, founded in 1867, reported on the latest fashions in New York shops—including French imports—and published a report by its Paris correspondent, Mme Raymond, as well as reporting on the activities of Parisian society. American women who could afford the tab commuted to Paris twice a year to choose their wardrobes for the following season, prompting a column which appeared from time to time, entitled "Those Dreadful Americans," satirizing their gaffes and general lack of sophistication.

French fashion magazines were all addressed to the bourgeoisie, whatever her financial level or social position, but they differed from each other in the specific segment of the public they wished to reach. *L'Art et la Mode* (1880–1967), which catered to the Parisienne, was the equivalent of *Harper's Bazar*, while the readers of *La Mode Illustrée*, writing from the provinces, wondered, "How is it that, even having dresses as beautiful as those of the parisiennes, we are not as well-dressed, as elegant, as they?" "I believe I can answer this question" replied Mme Raymond.

The proverbial elegance of the parisiennes is due above all to the important role they assign their petites robes. That is the designation used here for morning dresses, walking dresses, and, by extension, at-home dresses. Wealth being equal, a provincial will have . . . dresses costlier than those of a parisienne; on the other hand, an equally well-off parisienne will be more elegant, because she budgets a considerable part of her expenditures for the "little dress," which she wears every day. The little dress in fancy fabric, wool, in cloth, according to the season, but a little dress made well, according to the current fashion and lasting no longer than this fashion, alas! . . . ephemeral. The result of this difference in the allotment of expenditures made by the provincial making . . . a grand (perhaps too grand) toilette, condemns her, on one hand, to make that toilette last for too many years, and on the other, to be unable to wear it with the ease and tranquility which are evidence of being accustomed to it. Less expense for the very formal dresses one rarely wears, more for the little everyday dresses, and one will be as elegant far from Paris as in Paris itself.

Gabrielle Chanel had yet to invent the "little black dress," but the chic inherent in utter simplicity was already understood by the perceptive Emmeline Raymond. In 1879, condemning the absurd and extraordinarily ugly excesses of the current season, she suggested an alternative to her readers: "We can happily bring, on our own behalf, a little order to this chaos. We can wear black dresses, embroidered in black jet, without feeling ourselves obliged to adopt embroideries in metallic beads reproducing every color." The antithesis of Worth, whose clients were accustomed to change their splendid apparel several times a day, she recommended that a simple toilette be made in either black or a very dark color, which would make it suitable for every daytime occasion. Mme Raymond's belief in "economy in elegance" was epitomized by this proposal, which might well have been introduced by Chanel, to whom the same watchword applied, almost a half century later.

Frenchwomen in the provinces were not alone in noticing the chic of the Parisienne. In 1885, *Peterson's* magazine remarked, "The dress of a parisian woman is conceded, the world over, to be the most tasteful, because always the most appropriate, of any worn anywhere. . . . The chief point to note about the dress of a parisian woman, no matter what her station in life may be, is its appropriateness. She does not wear as costly garments usually as the American of the same social class, but they are always thoroughly suitable to her position and to the occasion on which they are worn."

Perhaps the most succinct observation regarding Parisian chic had been made over a century earlier by Jean-Jacques Rousseau: "Fashion dominates provincial women, but the parisiennes govern fashion, and know how to turn it to their own advantage. The first are like ignorant and servile plagiarists who copy even spelling errors; the latter are like authors who are master copiers and know how to correct mistakes in the original."

During the 1860s the ball gowns in *La Mode Illustrée* possessed an emphatically imperial air, (pages 24–25) with bands of lace crossed over the breast and a shoulder-hung court train. Originally designed by Worth in 1855 while he was still employed at Gagelin & Opigez, the court train appeared in Paris trade journals in 1868 and soon replaced the traditional train attached at the waist.

Empress Eugénie was the object of perpetual surveillance by the fashion press, which reported every detail of her wardrobe and christened garments "manteau Eugénie" or "peignoir imperatrice." Aside from Worth gowns, she manifested a fondness for the boleros of her native Spain and for the Scottish tartans of her mother's country. The popularity of fichus in the late 1850s and early 1860s (page 4) reflected her admiration for Marie

Antoinette. She owned a necklace of priceless pigeons'-blood rubies which had belonged to the hapless queen and even employed the architect Lefeul to design salons in the Tuileries in Louis XVI style.

The eclectism of the empress was not unique to her, but was a fundamental tenet of nineteenth-century style, which can best be characterized by its failure to develop an innate design vocabulary. This utter absence was concealed by an infinite number of adaptations of earlier styles—Greco-Roman, neoclassic, Gothic, Renaissance, and rococo. No other century borrowed so heavily from the past. A spate of revivals, historical novels, operas, political events, and international influences informs every area of nineteenth-century dress to varying degrees, from the chapeau Valois and the chapeau Berger which so captivated Mallarmé in *La Dernière Mode*, to the ubiquitous shawls from Kashmir and the Buffalo Bill hat (page 105) inspired by the appearance of William Cody's *Wild West Show* which opened the *Paris Exposition Universelle* in 1889. The completion of the Suez Canal in 1869 popularized Egyptian fashion (sortie de théâtre, page 32), while the burnous (page 23) was introduced due to French involvement in North Africa, and the Zouave jacket (page 5) and Garibaldi chemisette originated with Garibaldi's invasion of Sicily in 1860.

These remarkable pastiches sometimes made it difficult to distinguish fashionable dress from fancy dress, which enjoyed a tremendous vogue throughout the century. Both looked to the past for inspiration, and there were numerous books on historic dress; notably Racinet's six-volume *Le Costume Historique* (1888) and a new edition of Cesare Vecellio's sixteenth-century *Habiti Antichi* from Firmin-Didot, the publisher of *La Mode Illustrée*, which printed excerpts from the book in the early 1860s. Charles Worth shared the fascination. During his apprentice days in London, he was a frequent visitor to the National Gallery, cultivating a predilection for period costume that was to have a profound influence on his oeuvre.

In 1867 an English magazine commented, ". . . it seems like a costume for a *bal travisti*; but it is not so. It is the fashion of the day to copy more or less exactly the dress worn by celebrated women in another age, and our fashionable couturière will ask you in what *style* you wish to dress." A description by *Demorest's* special correspondent of a royal wedding at the church of La Madeleine in December, 1883, rife with period allusions, noted that the bride wore a dress with a Medici collar composed of tiny buds and blossoms, the groom's sister wore a blue moiré dress with a "broad Lamballe sash" and a tiny capote "in the Greek form," one princess wore a "Louis XVI costume of silver-gray satin richly brocaded," another topped off her smoke-gray velvet toilette with a "small capote in Tudor form," while yet another was dressed à la "Marie Antoinette." The Marquise of Castellane "was resplendent in a Rubens costume of Neapolitan coral velvet, and hat of Aurore velvet with silver ornaments."

At mid-century, the only sporting costumes depicted with any regularity were hunting and riding "amazon" apparel, their main attraction being their modishness. A hunting toilette acclaimed in *La Vie Parisienne*, 1874, not for its practicality, but for its seductiveness, was "of

hazelnut velvet, trimmed in bright green. The short skirt allows a glimpse of a foot, celebrated for its marvelous arch, shod in a high boot of hazelnut leather, laced with green ribbon. The bodice, fitted and very clinging, delineates a bust which seems modeled after that of the Venus of Florence. Over thick jet braids, and tilted toward light blue eyes framed by a long black fringe, a little hazelnut-colored felt with a large green feather. I tell you that dressed in this way, the pretty lady in question will be more seductive than in her sumptuous evening apparel."

In the latter half of the century, trains cut travel time from Paris to the beaches by two-thirds, and the popularity of recreational garb increased correspondingly. During the Second Empire, the trip from Paris to Dieppe, which had taken twelve hours by carriage, took only four hours by rail. Weekends on the Normandy coast were now possible, with spouses arriving on the "husbands' train." In August 1854, *Le Figaro*, noting the oppressive heat and emptiness of Paris, observed, "every living thing has apparently sought refuge on the railway platforms." The Touring Club of France initiated organized leisure activities in 1890 and the *Guide Michelin* followed suit in 1900. The railroad permitted the development of tourism, and suitable clothing followed. Leisure garb, encompassing travel and sportswear, became a major category of apparel, and the sole area of dress owing nothing to the past.

British tailoring formed the basis for sportswear, and, since practicality was a prime requisite, function overrode fantasy. The English firm of Redfern was responsible for the tailored suit consisting of jacket, skirt, and shirtwaist, worn by women on both sides of the Atlantic. Originally makers of mourning clothes, Redfern was founded at Cowes, on the Isle of Wight, where the Prince of Wales spent the yachting season. The firm began to make yachting apparel, and its first success was the wool jersey costume worn by Lillie Langtry in 1879. A waterproof fabric made of rubber between two layers of cloth had already been developed by Macintosh in 1823, while Burberry, ca. 1880, invented gabardine, a cotton waterproofed prior to being woven; these two fabrics were to have widespread use in sportswear.

Besides spending time at the seashore and spas in leisurely pursuits, women began to play tennis, ride bicycles, hike, and swim. Resorts featured racetracks and casinos where clothing could be displayed to advantage. This led to a transformation in the kind of apparel featured in *La Mode Illustrée*, and by 1890 a marked increase in casual and resort dress for day and evening was evident. The word *villégiature*, defined by Larousse as "a recreational sojourn in the country," enjoyed frequent usage as a designation for vacation daywear.

The heavy upholstery styles of the '80s and early '90s, in such somber colors as brun Eiffel, were, judging by the settings in which they were customarily depicted, destined for indoor wear. Supplanted by the filmy ruffles and flounces so fashionable during the Belle Époque, neither fashion ever invaded sportswear. Fashion plates picture women at resorts side by side in both types of apparel, copious amounts of lace encircling white shoulders and cascading down beguiling toilettes which share the page with women in starched sailor dresses.

No fashion magazine, nor any fashion for that matter, exists in a vacuum. To learn what a society is about, one need only look at the illustrations in its fashion periodicals. *La Mode Illustrée* provides a panoramic view of the change in attitudes toward women from 1860 to 1914. Its earliest plates, showing women in crinoline-supported skirts, present a sloped-shouldered, submissive view of femininity enhanced by downcast eyes under demure bonnets or hats, barely visible tiny feet, and children clinging to their mothers' skirts, in an interior redolent of blissful domesticity or a carefully tended, cloistered garden. Men and women inhabited separate spheres, with the home being woman's domain. Hence, the total absence of men in the plates before the 1880s, when an occasional man made an appearance, usually in such at-home garb as a bathrobe or smoking jacket. A retrospective look at fashion from the fiftieth anniversary issue in 1909 makes a telling statement continually borne out by the plethora of needlework projects which were a regular feature of *La Mode Illustrée*, as well as by an 1877 fashion plate (page 49):

> Returning home, the *comme il faut* woman does not fail to put on her apron, symbol of domestic virtue and indispensible complement to the at home toilette: moreover, a very elegant taffeta apron trimmed with fringe, ruches or lace. She places on her hair a headdress of blonde lace decorated with velvet twists, tassels, or pinked edges. Thus the woman, the young girl, appear to us, hardworking and caring, guardians of the home, holding in their hands the tapestry slippers or the velvet cap they are embroidering for their father or spouse!

In 1884, *Godey's* heralded women's emergence from indoors to outdoors, noting that "there were [now] two kinds of prevailing styles: the newer 'tailor-made' fashions and the older 'couturier-made' apparel." (Lois W. Banner, *American Beauty*, 1983) During the Belle Époque, the plates in *La Mode Illustrée* portrayed women at resorts, chateaux, and balls. They hiked, rowed boats, rode bicycles, and appeared about to play golf and tennis. Around 1900, replete with dusters and goggles, they climbed into open automobiles.

> The ambition of the modern woman is to show herself everywhere. She is no longer content with the drawing-room, the ballroom, and theatre; she must reign in the open air; and sports have been invented—croquet, skating, and lawn tennis—in which she can mix with men and dwarf them . . . picnics have become the rage; water-parties and walking-tours exhibit woman's taste in fancy costumes, and her powers of hand and foot, for she does not disdain to pull an oar, and will back herself for a "discretion" to walk long distances. . . . (James Laver, *Manners and Morals in the Age of Optimism, 1848–1914*, 1966)

By 1912, holidays were so ubiquitous that *La Revue Hebddomadaire* was moved to remark, "Fifty years ago the person who took a vacation stood out. Today a person stands out who does not take a vacation." As women began to participate in outdoor sports and travel on trains or ships, tailored clothing, albeit equipped with fashionable accoutrements such as bustles, became an important part of the wardrobe. Nonetheless, formal garb was still made of lavishly trimmed, heavy fabrics with cumbersome trains. With the spread of higher education, and an increase in the number of women working outside the home, ready-made suits and tailor-made suits with skirts short enough for climbing on trams accounted for an important part of the apparel business in the United States. Redfern, suit-maker to Princess Alexandra, claimed the superiority of male tailors over dressmakers, and opened branches in London, Paris, New York, and Chicago. "In 1893, *Harper's Weekly* noted that the 'evolution of sensible dress' had kept pace with women's expanded participation in colleges, in the professions, and in the work force. The magazine defined sensible dress as the 'blazer suit,' consisting of a narrow skirt, what is called a 'shirt-front' blouse, and a comfortable jacket." (Banner, *American Beauty*.) Significantly, the suit incorporated masculine elements such as menswear fabrics, starched collars, pleated shirt fronts and cravats.

Easily as important a factor in the change in lifestyles as train travel and the establishment of resorts was the adoption in the late 1880s of the new safety bicycle equipped with two wheels of equal size and pneumatic tires. Its popularity was instantaneous, and, in the '90s, an annual bicycle exhibition was held at the Palais de l'Industrie, while the French Army trained a bicycle corps in the belief that it could virtually replace the cavalry in wartime, even fitting out cycles with rapid-firing machine guns. By 1895, there were close to two million cyclists in America, forty thousand of them women. Not only could women now wear costumes that allowed them freedom of movement, the bicycle provided a means of un-precedented mobility. Sarah Bernhardt believed that the bicycle would transform mores more profoundly than was generally believed. She saw in all those young girls pedalling outdoors a renunciation in large measure of domesticity and family life. The bicycling craze was universal: Americans returning from Paris, where they saw society leaders cycling in the Bois de Boulogne, rode in Newport, Bar Harbor, and Southampton in the summer, while fashion magazines devoted innumerable pages to cycling apparel and bloomer versus skirt. The *Illustrated American* declared New York women con-servative to the point of frumpiness compared to Paris, where "one sees the grandes dames and the cocottes on the wheel clad alike, and bloomers reign supreme, until a skirt appears quite in the light of a novelty, so rarely is one seen," and where even Maison Worth was designing cycling bloomers. The Paris edition of the *New York Herald* believed that, "a fashion paper dealing exclusively with sporting costumes might sustain the interest of its weekly readers from one end of the year to the other." More important than what was considered proper attire was the implication that women could leave home on their bicycles, for work or pleasure. A daring concept, it was underscored by the act of riding astride, as yet hazarded by few equestriennes.

Reflecting the new attitudes, fashion emphasis shifted in the late 80s to the shoulders, which inflated to full-blown balloons by 1895, presenting an imposing silhouette not unlike that of 1860 turned upside-down. It was no coincidence that an assertive effect had become fashionable. The broadening of women's horizons in the latter part of the century was reshaping their view of themselves, and sports transformed their view of feminine beauty. The demure lady of the 1860s had finally become a woman, and the fashions of the succeeding years emphasized her modernity.

A corollary to these changes concerned a new attitude toward aging. The fiftieth anniversary issue of *La Mode Illustrée*, in a retrospective of fashion, remarked that since the advent of the new century, "one can dress as she wishes and wear her hair as she desires. Age itself is freed from narrow and uncomfortable constraints. No longer, as in the past, are youth and age each assigned appropriate fashions. Tolerance, on this point, increases. Women do not wish to grow old and one learns not to be astonished to see granddaughter and grandmother wearing the same toilettes, the same hats, and partaking of the same pleasures." Clothing deemed "comme il faut" for the middle-aged, the woman of "a certain age," and the elderly lady did not cease to appear; however, this apparel was becoming almost indistinguishable from the fashions created for the readers of *La Mode Illustrée*, who probably ranged in age from twenty to thirty-five.

Typical of the fashion advice proffered at the turn of the century, an article in the January 1900 *Ladies' Home Journal*, "The Dress of the Business Girl" ("who must be prepared to go out in all sorts of weather") counseled that "the first thing to consider in her wardrobe is the business suit." Mme Raymond concurred. Women of all stations in life should have the ability to provide for themselves, in cases where they might not marry or where a misfortune might deny them the support of a husband's income. She wrote, "I have never understood the feminist doctrine: but I hold the firm conviction that a well-advised feminism would guide women towards this goal, which would represent independence, if they had to live alone, or to help, if they are called on to create a family." Believing it was no longer enough to paint a fan or a lampshade in a gifted amateur manner, or to sing or play the piano pleasingly enough to attract a few pupils, she felt that serious study was becoming indispensible. Her aspirations were pitifully modest however: when advising parents to encourage their little girls' aptitudes (February 11, 1900), she wrote that if a child fashions the hats of her doll cleverly, "it is down that path that she should be guided and made to learn the trade of milliner . . . At these words, one may be slightly outraged . . . Why? If she has no need to practice her metier, she will have the advantage of saving the expense of a milliner; moreover, she will have the enjoyment of executing work which is said to be highly amusing. There are millionaires who make their own hats . . . for the pleasure of making them."

"Is the little girl adept at making dolls' clothes?" She should be taught the trade of dressmaker. Nonetheless, Mme Raymond agreed with conservative contemporaries such as the writer who believed, "You can't all paint pictures or carve statues or write books, but you can learn how to be wise, competent, firm, tender mothers. You can paint pictures on little brains, carve statues in little characters, write books in little lives whose influence will live forever. Such a career would make men count you a greater woman than if your image were to be found worthy to fill a niche in the Hall of Fame. . . . If all the successful women in the world; all the women who have risen to the top of their respective arts or crafts, could send one word and message to all the women who yearn after a public career, that one word would be 'Don't' and the message would be 'Try to find contentment in your own lot, for we do not find it here.'" (Lillian Bell, *Why Men Remain Bachelors and Other Luxuries*, 1906)

In spite of an acknowledgment of the need for simpler dress, fashion's foundation remained the corseted shape in favor at the time. At the turn of the century, even sportswear was defined by an S-shaped corset that forced the bosom forward and the hips backward, glorifying the full-blown woman. The feathers, lace, and froufrou of dressy clothes bespoke attraction and seduction. Even underclothing was made in pastel silks and trimmed with copious amounts of lace, inspiring a book, *The Cult of Chiffon* (Mrs. Eric Pritchard, 1902). Toward the end of the decade, the designer Paul Poiret freed woman from her ruffled chrysalis, and she emerged upright and sleek in a long corset that bypassed her waist and narrowed her hips. Inspired by the Orient and the Ballets Russes, which made its Paris debut in 1909, Poiret transformed women into mysterious creatures arrayed in brilliantly-hued hobble skirts and draped tunics, more attuned to the rhythm of the tango than the waltz. A talented promoter as well as a gifted designer, he was to be as powerful a force as Worth, imposing his perception of fashion on the world and spawning a host of imitators whose garments all bore the unmistakable stamp of Poiret, in some cases literally, with the use of counterfeit labels. He served as a bridge between the unrestrained opulence of the nineteenth century and the understated elegance of the twentieth, but his reign was brief, declining with the ascendance of Chanel after World War I.

While evening dress evoked lush Oriental imagery, daytime apparel was paring down, accommodating itself to a world in which the pace was accelerated by the motor car and the Métro, and in which there was no longer time to change clothes several times a day. In February 1912, *Les Modes* remarked on the vogue for plain dresses "of relatively simple execution, whose simplicity of line is a trifle too uniform, so quickly imposed that they seem to have emerged all at once from a single mold." Fans and parasols were replaced by handbags and umbrellas. The tailleur or "tout-aller" costume could be donned in the morning and worn until dinner, prefiguring Chanel's declaration: "Fashion is at once both a caterpillar and butterfly. Be a caterpillar by day and a butterfly by night. Nothing could be more comfortable than a caterpillar and nothing more made for love than a butterfly. There must be dresses that crawl and dresses that fly. The butterfly does not go to market, and the caterpillar does not go to a ball."

Just as the railroad superseded the horse and carriage, in the years immediately prior to World War I both were replaced by the automobile, and the pattern of life changed yet again.

> The sound of the horn has replaced the crack of the whip, the pneumatic tire has taken the place of the bandage metallique, and the chauffeur that of the coachman. One does not compare bloodlines any more, but horsepower. No longer does one take pride in sparkling harness, but concern about the luxury of carriagework.

And if some god grants us the leisure of a short vacation, and we have the desire to take an attractive trip, we no longer think about taking the train, an impersonal mode of transport, authoritarian and somewhat outmoded. We go forth, comfortably installed in an auto, allowing ourselves to follow our fancies. The roads seem to open up before us, offering their picturesque and varied aspects which seduce us according to our mood of the moment. Free to stop at a charming place which pleases us, to leave again when our caprice dictates, to take a right turn because, down there, the banks of a river enchant us, or to the left, because the view of the valley must be exquisite; we can abandon the great centers for the delicious corners that we discover; unknown corners of which we would always have remained in ignorance without our blessed automobiles. (*Les Modes*, October 1913, "Chronique des Sports")

This new, private manner of travel, spontaneous and informal, further changed the face of sportswear. Touring the countryside required comfortable shoes and sweaters, and, in the not too distant future, slacks for women. The new style, in a phrase to be coined by Mainbocher in the 1930s, was "spectator sportswear," meant to be worn all day for work or leisure. Loose fitting jackets with raglan sleeves, shorter skirts with pleats allowing their wearers to take long strides, and coat sweaters appeared with increasing frequency in *La Mode Illustrée* from 1912 on. In short, the magazine's subscribers had been transformed into twentieth-century women, dressed for the demands of a life which was to prove very different from that of their mothers. They had only to await the ominous sound of war in the summer of 1914, for an opportunity to use their skills in offices and factories when called into the labor force to replace men drafted into active service.

There was no turning back. The groundwork had been laid for Chanel's generation to complete the metamorphosis by designing minimal, uncomplicated clothes that incorporated functionalism with youthful grace and freedom of movement, severing all ties with the historical allusions of nineteenth-century dress and paring away its remaining complexities to influence the whole of the twentieth. It is extraordinary to reflect on the magnitude of change in fashion during the fifty-four years from the founding of *La Mode Illustrée*, when Worth dictated fashion, to the onset of the First World War. Poiret reigned over the brilliant nocturnal butterflies of pre-war Paris, but it was the young Chanel who understood that the caterpillar was the key to the future of fashion. She said, "I was in attendance at the death of luxury, at the demise of the nineteenth century, and also at the end of an era. . . . A world was dying while another was being born. I was there, an opportunity came forward, and I took it. I was the same age as the new century, and it was to me that it looked for sartorial expression."

Glossary

Aigrette: Upright tuft of feathers; something resembling a feather aigrette.

Alpaca: Shiny plain-weave fabric with silk or cotton warp and alpaca filling.

Armure: Fabric with a pebbly surface, sometimes with a repeat design or small motifs.

Astrakhan: Pile-weave fabric imitating Persian lamb or broadtail fur.

Basque: Small peplum.

Basquine: Woman's coat or jacket.

Batavia: Lightweight, twill-weave silk fabric.

Batiste: High-quality, soft, lightweight cotton fabric.

Bavolet: Flounce falling from the rear of a bonnet concealing the back of the neck.

Bayadère: Crosswise multicolored stripes; fabric with such stripes.

Bengaline: Heavy ribbed silk with a corded effect.

Bertha: Piece of fabric bordering the neckline of a bodice, or a collar placed on a wide neckline, usually of equal width all around.

Blonde: Silk lace that may be either white or black.

Boa: Long round scarf, often of fur or feathers.

Bolero: Waist or rib-length jacket, with or without sleeves.

Bottine: Short boot.

Bouillonné: Shirred band of fabric.

Bretelles: Shoulder straps attached to a waistband, either decorative or actually supporting a skirt.

Brocade: Fabric with a satin-weave design on a plain-, satin-, or rib-weave background.

Broderie anglaise: Eyelet embroidery.

Burnous: Sleeveless evening wrap with a hood.

Cabochon: Stone cut in a round convex shape without facets.

Casaque: Three-quarter length, loose-fitting outer garment, often open-sided and with slit sleeves, sometimes trimmed with braid.

Cashmere: Fine, soft dress fabric made from the wool of Kashmir goats.

Chamois: Soft, pliable leather.

Changeable moiré: Fabric with warp of one color and woof of another, giving different effect in different lights.

Chantilly lace: Type of bobbin lace.

Charmeuse: Lightweight, lustrous dress fabric of cotton or silk.

Chemise: A loose gown, falling straight down from shoulders to hem.

Chemisette: A sleeveless vestee or dickey made of fine cotton, lace, or net, used primarily to fill low necklines.

Chenille: Fabric made of a silk, cotton, or wool yarn with pile protruding all around.

Cheviot: Close-napped, rough-surfaced, twill-weave wool fabric used for suits and coats.

Chicoree: Manner of cutting fabric with a pinked edge, similar to a chicory leaf, and leaving it unhemmed; also a ruche formed from strips of fabric cut in this fashion.

Chignon: Twist of hair forming a bun, worn at the back of the head.

Chinchilla: Blue-gray fur.

Cloche: Hat with bell-shaped crown.

Coiffure: Hair style or headdress.

Collarette: Small collar, especially of lace, fur, beads, etc.

Combinations: Chemise-pantaloons or petticoat-pantaloons.

Combing jacket or *sacque:* Loose jacket worn over lingerie while making toilette.

Confection: Ready-to-wear garment, usually referring to outerwear.

Corselet: Lightly boned corset.

Coutil: A sturdy, twill-woven cotton, used for corsets.

Covert-cloth: Durable, medium-weight, twill-weave fabric, having a finely speckled appearance; used for suits, coats, and riding habits.

Crepe: Fabric with a grained or crinkled surface; can be made of silk, cotton, wool, etc.

Crepe de chine: Fine silk crepe.

Crepe-chiffon: Sheer silk crepe.

Crepeline: Sheer, lustrous or semi-lustrous, wool, silk, or cotton dress fabric with a crepe effect.

Crepon: Heavy crepe fabric.

Dagged: Cut into points, leaves, or scallops along the edge.

Damask: Reversible fabric, woven in floral or geometric patterns.

Décolletage: Neckline.

Demi-boot: Ankle boot.

Dentelé: Notched or scalloped.

Diadem: Headpiece resembling a crown.

Duster: Lightweight coat worn to protect clothing.

Duvetyn: Soft, twill-weave wool with a nap.

En échelle: Applied decoration, often of ribbons, simulating ladder of ribbon on a stomacher.

Epaulettes: Shoulder ornaments.

Ermine: White fur with black-tipped tails.

Etamine: Lightweight, loosely woven plain-weave cotton or worsted fabric.

Fagoting: Thread, ribbon, or braid used straight or criss-crossed in an open seam to form an openwork trimming.

Faille: Finely ribbed silk, cotton, or wool.

Fanchon: Knitted or crocheted head scarf.

Fedora: Low felt hat with a soft, medium-width brim and a lengthwise crease in the crown.

Fichu: Scarf covering neck and shoulders and tied with ends over the chest or tucked into the decolletage, made of a filmy silk or cotton muslin, worn by Marie Antoinette in the 1780s and popular at various times in the nineteenth century.

Figaro jacket: Waist or rib-length jacket.

Flounce: Gathered or pleated strip of fabric sewn to a garment; one edge is generally left free.

Foulard: Fine soft silk or cotton in a twill weave, often printed in a small design.

Frog: Looped fastener made of braid or cord.

Garniture: Decorative trimming.

Gauze: Light, loosely-woven, transparent fabric of cotton, silk, or linen.

Gilet: Sleeveless bodice with a decorative front worn in place of a blouse.

Glacé: Surface finished with a glossy, highly polished effect.

Grosgrain: Fabric or ribbon with heavy ribs.

Guimpe: Short chemise of lightweight material to fill in low-necked or open bodices.

Guipure: Various large-patterned heavy laces, the motifs connected by brides instead of a net ground.

Horsehair: Stiff, loosely-woven fabric made from the hair of a horse; used for stiffening.

Insertion: Narrow lace or embroidery with plain edges set into a fabric as decoration.

Jabot: Frill or ruffle, often of lace, fastened at the neckline and falling down the front of the bodice.

Jersey: Plain-knit fabric, usually of wool.

Latticework: Openwork decoration made by crossing narrow strips of fabric, ribbon, lace, braid, etc.

Lorgnette: Eyeglasses on an ornamental handle.

Maline: Gauze-like net of silk or cotton.

Manteau: Overcoat or greatcoat.

Mantelet: Outer garment similar to a shawl made with some tailoring.

Marabou: Soft tail and wing feathers of the stork.

Marten: Soft, fine fur.

Mary Stuart headdress: Headdress with a heart-shaped peak projecting over the center of the forehead.

Matinée: A morning wrapper.

Medici collar: Large, fan-shaped standing collar.

Merino: Fine, soft, dress fabric made from the wool of the merino sheep.

Merveilleux: A silk or silk/cotton mixture in a twill weave with a lustrous finish.

Mohair: Fabric made of the long, lustrous, silky hair of the Angora goat.

Moiré: Stiff, ribbed silk-and-cotton fabric with a watered effect.

Mousseline: Muslin.

Mousseline de soie: A fine silk with a gauzy muslin weave.

Muff: Pillow-like covering for the hands.

Muslin: Plain-weave cotton.

Nainsook or *nainsouk:* A thin, delicate, plain-weave cotton.

Ombré: Graduated in color.

Organdy: Crisp, fine muslin, slightly stiffened.

Ottoman: Firm, plain, heavy fabric with crosswise ribs.

Paillette: Flat, glittering disk sewn onto fabric as decoration; spangle.

Paletot: Loose jacket or short overcoat, usually with sleeves.

Panné velvet: Velvet with flattened pile.

Pannier: A structure or device worn at the sides to extend the hips. Also, a portion of a skirt arranged to provide fullness at the sides.

Pardessus: Literally, overcoat. A general term for outer garments in the nineteenth century including mantelets, visites, paletots, etc. Used to describe men's sleeved paletots in the latter part of the century.

Passementerie: Applied trimmings such as braids, cords, and heavy embroideries.

Peau-de-soie or *poult-de-soie:* A very fine, corded silk.

Pelerine: Cape or cloak of varying lengths.

Pelisse: Long cloak.

Percale: Firm, plain-weave cotton fabric.

Piqué: Firm fabric with a lengthwise corded effect.

Plastron: V-shaped front of a woman's costume.

Plissé: Gathered or pleated.

Plush: Rich fabric with longer pile than velvet.

Point d'esprit: Net or tulle with dots.

Polonaise: A coat-gown with the fronts of the skirts pulled back over an underskirt.

Pompon: Small ball of wool, feathers, ribbon, etc. worn as an ornament.

Poplin: Fabric woven with silk warp and wool or worsted filling, with a finely corded surface.

Porte-jupe: A belt, worn under the dress, with suspenders for looping up the outer skirt;

Poult-de-soie: See *peau-de-soie.*

Princesse: A gown shaped from shoulder to hem without a seam at the waist.

Raglan sleeve: Sleeve with long armhole line extending to neckline.

Ratiné: Cloth made with nub yarns to produce a rough surface.

Redingote: Originally a man's riding coat, it is a long gown, fitted at the waist, and open down the front, worn over a skirt.

Reps: Fabric with closely spaced ribs running in the direction of the weft.

Reticule: Pouch bag with a drawstring top.

Revers: Lapel; also a turn-back on a sleeve or skirt.

Rosette: Ribbon decoration formed in the shape of a rose.

Rouleau: Roll or fold of fabric.

Ruche: A narrow pleated or shirred edging made of lace, net, or matching fabric of dress.

Sacque: Loose jacket.

Scallop: A circular curve, made in series along an edge.

Serge: Soft, durable, woolen fabric.

Shantung: Plain-weave fabric with irregular slubs, usually silk.

Shirred: Gathered.

Sicilienne: A fine poplin with silk warp and cashmere filling.

Snood: Heavy mesh net worn at the back of the head to confine the hair.

Sortie de bal: Outer garment worn over evening or ball dresses.

Soutache: Narrow decorative braid.

Spencer jacket: Tight-fitting short jacket.

Strass: Substance used in making costume jewelry.

Surah: A soft twilled silk or wool, similar to foulard but heavier.

Swansdown: Fine, soft underfeathers of swans, used as trimming.

Tabbed: Having a border of loose-hanging pieces of fabric with square or round edges.

Tablier: An apron effect, usually draped, on the front of a skirt.

Taffeta: Glossy silk fabric with a plain weave.

Talma: Long circular cape.

Tarlatan: A kind of thin, stiff, transparent muslin.

Tassel: An ornament with threads or cords hanging in a loose fringe.

Toque: Small, close-fitting, brimless hat.

Tortoiseshell: Mottled brown-and-yellow covering on the shell of some kinds of turtles; used in making accessories.

Tournure: Bustle.

Tulle: Fine net.

Valenciennes: Fine bobbin lace in which the same thread forms both the ground and the design.

Velours: Closely woven, smooth fabric with nap.

Veloutine: Corded wool dress fabric with a velvety finish.

Vestee: An imitation vest or blouse front worn under a dress or jacket.

Vicuna: Soft fabric made from the wool of the vicuña, a llama-like animal from South America.

Visite: Jacket closely fitting the body, with sleeves tight-fitting to the elbow, widening below.

Voile: Fine, transparent or semi-transparent plain-weave fabric of cotton, silk, rayon, or wool.

Wrapper: Loose, informal garment for casual wear.

Zephyr: Very lightweight fabric.

Zouave jacket: Woman's short, military-style jacket.

1   2   3   4

1. Little girl's toilette. Dress of bright blue poplin. Manteau of orange-and-black striped Algerian fabric. Hat trimmed with black velvet and matching feathers. **2.** Little girl's toilette. Black taffeta dress. The flounces are edged with a band of plaid taffeta. The bodice is trimmed front and back en échelle, with plaid taffeta bands. Wide black ribbon sash bound in plaid taffeta. **3.** Taffeta redingote, buttoned from neck to hem. Mantelet of embroidered black tulle. Round hat for the country, lined in green taffeta edged with black velvet and trimmed with green and black pheasant feathers. **4.** Dress of violet poult-de-soie. The skirt is trimmed with three ruches *à la vieille*. The bodice is pointed; the sleeves, extremely wide, are trimmed with a ruche *à la vieille*. Hat of pale green ribbed velvet with a pleated brim and a white blonde lace facing; trim of white and green feathers. The coiffure is composed of hair waved slightly off the face and puffed out by the waviness of the hair itself, without the aid of pads.

1. Young lady's toilette. Dress of blue-and-black striped taffeta. The skirt is trimmed with a wide flounce, surmounted by two narrow ruffles; a double ruche is placed above the narrow ruffles. The décolleté bodice is trimmed with a fichu with rounded ends, edged with a double ruche; white muslin sleeves; high-necked pleated muslin chemisette. Round straw hat. 2. Dress of buff foulard, trimmed with six flounces topped by a narrow bouillonné; the jacket fronts and neck edging are trimmed with two bands of shirring; the sash and the bows on the jacket are of black velvet. The collar is a shirred band of white muslin, threaded with a ribbon.

1. Little boy's suit. Blouse and pants of black-and-white striped poplin with black soutache trim. 2. Autumn redingote of gray taffeta. Each width of fabric is scalloped along its entire length in brown silk with a button in every scallop, and each overlaps the next panel. The bodice is also scalloped in front, as are the cuffs and the sleeve seams. 3. Dress of violet poult-de-soie. A two-tone violet ruche edges the black guipure along the sides of the skirt, on the bodice, and the sleeves. Passementerie buttons of two shades of violet encircled by guipure are placed in the space between the ruches.

1

2   3   4

1. Marie Antoinette fichu, front and back views. 2. Taffeta Lavallière bonnet in two shades of brown, embroidered in chenille; trimmed with velvet flowers and a bunch of grapes. It is encircled by black lace; black velvet ribbon strings. The interior is trimmed with the same flowers. 3. Mexican blue satin bonnet. The brim is black satin, appliquéd with black velvet leaves whose veins are indicated by black beads. The bavolet, matching the brim, is trimmed with wide lace. A black aigrette adorns the crown, the brim facing is trimmed with feathers and velvet flowers of Mexican blue. The strings are black taffeta with lace edging. 4. White velvet bonnet with full bavolet of green velvet, edged with black lace; the top of the hat is embellished with a large green velvet bow trimmed with pink flowers and black berries; brim facing matches; wide white bonnet strings, second set in black lace.

1. Net sleeve with bouillonnés separated by ribbons. 2. Child's white taffeta bonnet trimmed with soutache and fringe. 3. White piqué child's bonnet. 4. Net sleeve trimmed with black and white lace, edged with black velvet. 5. Dress for a one- to two-year-old child. Low-necked bodice with bretelles attached to the belt. A chemisette trimmed with embroidery and lace is worn underneath. 6. Dress for a two-year-old child, of nainsouk, piqué, or wool, with soutache trim. 7. Christening dress trimmed with lace and broderie anglaise. 8. Chemisette with sailor collar in muslin, trimmed with lace. 9. White muslin chemisette trimmed with a bouillonné in the shape of a cravat. 10. Christening bonnet trimmed with lace ruches and small ribbon bouquets. 11. Bonnet for one-year-old child. Embroidered ground, embroidery insertions, lace ruches, and ribbon bows. 12. Shirred white bodice with bands of stitching and insertions. 13. Chemisette with heart-shaped neckline edged with net bouillonné framed with ribbon. 14. Zouave jacket.

1. Dress with corselet for little girl age eight to ten, front and back views. **2.** Costume for little boy age three to four, front and back views. **3.** Costumes and outerwear from Maison Pauline Royer, rue de Rivoli.

1–3. Three straw chapeaux. **4.** Boot! . . . Yes, a boot for a lady, in Russian leather, with black and white silk stitching; black buttons and fringe of tiny bells. **5.** Checkerboard bottine in gray and black leather, patent leather upper. **6.** Lady's boot of brown morocco leather, patent upper, brown silk cord laces. **7.** Violet velvet slipper, gray satin revers; violet silk cord rosette. **8.** Black velvet slipper, red plush lining, red silk cord rosette and piping. **9.** Bottine of kidskin, patent leather, and jet ball-button trim. **10.** Black grosgrain slipper, checkerboard revers of light gray and violet satin, black chenille rosette. **11.** Bottine of black Turkish satin, gray leather trim imitating leaves and flowers.

1

2

Seaside costumes. **1.** White piqué dress trimmed with a wide lilac piqué band on the front of the skirt, embroidered in black soutache and surrounded by a chicoree ruche of black taffeta. The bodice, with a small basque, has a lilac piqué plastron embroidered and trimmed like the skirt. The sleeve trim matches the dress. Round hat of white muslin tubing, lilac ribbon trim. **2.** Skirt of ecru-and-black striped taffeta, trimmed with a band of black taffeta with soutache embroidery, and framed by a ruche of black taffeta ribbon. Fitted jacket of ecru taffeta and black soutache, trimmed with ruches and plastron of the same material as the skirt. The lower corners of the jacket are folded back, as are those of the sleeves, which are slit to the elbow. Hood of ecru batiste trimmed with taffeta ruches. Bouffant embroidered blouse, held by a wide black taffeta sash.

Bathing costumes. **1.** Wide trousers in blue wool; blouse and a kind of casaque with cape collar in blue-and-black striped wool; black wool braid covers all the seams. Round hat of matching blue wool. **2.** Heavy white merino trousers and jacket trimmed with black wool braid; embroidered anchors in the corners. Round hat in white cashmere. **3.** Trousers and skirt of black wool with red; red bands and sash; red blouse-bodice; hairnet of red wool, lined with black ciré (oilskin). **4.** Trousers, skirt, and jacket in blue wool taffeta with black wool braid trim; short sleeves. Bonnet-snood in blue cashmere with black cashmere bow.

1   2

Toilettes by Madame Vignon-Chauvin, rue de Rivoli. **1.** Green taffeta dress. The skirt has a black taffeta border with a scalloped upper edge, topped by two black taffeta bands whose ends cross the medallion above each scallop of the wide band. High-necked bodice. Swiss belt of black taffeta. The decoration on the bodice matches the skirt. Elbow-length sleeves trimmed as the skirt. Undersleeves in white muslin to the wrist. **2.** Young lady's toilette. Skirt of blue mousseline de soie, trimmed with three bands of black taffeta. High-necked plissé bodice and sleeves of white muslin. Petit bodice of black taffeta, black velvet edging and bretelles. Headdress of black velvet, trimmed with pink roses. This toilette may be worn at a soirée or an official dinner.

1   2

1. Town toilette. Dress in violet poult-de-soie, with matching pardessus; black chenille embroidery trim. White satin hat, with bavolet and trim of violet velvet. **2.**
Traveling toilette. Dress of steel gray wool poplin. The skirt is trimmed with a band
of black, white, and violet plaid. Wide matching cloak edged with wool chenille
fringe. Round hat of black velvet, with white, black, and violet feathers, held by a
black velvet rosette.

Ball and evening toilettes by Mme Alexandre Ghys, rue Sainte-Anne.

1   2

1. Dress of white mohair with mauve stripes. Two dentelé bands, edged with a fluted ruffle, trim the hem of the skirt and *rise en tablier;* the front panel is trimmed with matching bands. Hat of white horsehair, with mauve taffeta lining and ties. **2.** Dress of white mohair, embroidered in silk braid of brown flecked with white. The dress, made in princesse style, closes with large buttons of brown antique moiré.

1

2

Toilettes by Mlle Castel, rue Sainte-Anne. **1.** Dress of steel gray mohair, trimmed with ball fringe in the same shade. Basquine bodice with simulated vest and elbow-length sleeves. High-necked nainsook chemisette with long sleeves. **2.** Dress of gooseberry taffeta, trimmed with latticework embroidery in black chenille, framed by black ball fringe. Bodice with basque open in front, with the same embroidery as the skirt; also on the sleeves.

1

1. Paletot Garde-Française. Model by Mme Gérard, rue du Faubourg-Saint-Honoré. Dark gray wool velours, with piping and revers of bright blue taffeta; gray leather belt, cording and tassels in bright blue silk, gray passementerie buttons. **2.** Bodice à la Grecque.

1–3. Summer chapeaux from Mme Aubert, rue Neuve-des-Mathurins. 1. Toque polonaise in straw, black velvet ribbon edging and large bow with streamers, a spray of oak leaves in front. 2. Italian straw hat with low brim front and back, edged with a ruche of brilliant blue velvet and white bells, a beaded butterfly holding a large white feather swept to the back over the crown. 3. Scottish toque in English straw, Mexican blue velvet trim, loops, and streamers. In front, a steel star ornament holding a blue ostrich feather. 4. Snood of Mexican blue silk floss with black taffeta ribbon threaded with elastic, covered with blue taffeta ribbon edging and bow. 5. Dress raised with a skirt elevator (porte-jupe). 6. Hat of white horsehair woven in diamonds, edged with a ruche of straw and horsehair, with tiny tubular beads of white jet; lace snood; reeds, sprigs of daisies, tiny glass berries. White taffeta ribbons.

1

2

Winter outerwear from the Magasins du Louvre, rue de Rivoli. **1.** Black velvet paletot, richly trimmed with passementerie and lace; this trim follows the edges of the paletot and the seams, draws a kind of frame along the front ends, and is repeated on the sleeves. **2.** White wool velours sortie de bal. The trim consists of narrow black velvet, pale gold braid, and silk fringes. The sortie de bal also available in red velours with the same trim as above. **3.** Bright blue wool casaque with tabs and braids of passementerie suitable for the dressy toilettes of a

3   4   5

young lady, as well as a morning toilette for a lady. **4.** *The Elegant.* Black velvet pardessus, trimmed with lace and passementerie. The trim simulates revers in the back, marks pockets, and is repeated on the sleeves, the shoulders, and the neck. **5.** *The Sportsman.* Paletot in white wool velours, with blue velours trim, white cording sparingly mixed with gold; blue velours buttons and hood trim; the large tassel ornament is blue, white, and gold silk cord. The same model is available in red wool velours.

From Magasins du Louvre. **1–2.** Chapeaux. **3.** Rodolphe paletot. **4.** Spring paletot.

1. Hood with collar. 2. Chapeau with tabbed edging. 3 & 5. Bouffant coiffure with plaited chignon by M. Croisat. 4. Bayadère headdress without veil. 6. Toque for traveling and the country. 7. Bayadère headdress from Mme Aubert, rue Laffitte. 8. Swedish toque for young lady.

Toilettes by Mme Bréant-Castel, rue des Petits-Champs. **1.** Violet cashmere petticoat. Dress and paletot in flecked gray wool. The dress is the same length as the petticoat except on the sides; its hem is trimmed with a ruffle and violet silk cording. Black velvet hat, black and white feathers. **2.** Petticoat, dress, and paletot of brown poplin. All the edges are dagged and piped in black taffeta. **3.** Petticoat, dress, and paletot of violet silk, with appliqués of black velvet sewn with white chalk beads.

1. Burnous for the seaside. Lined white wool, with orange cashmere banding, fringe, and embroidery. **2.** Cashmere shawl. The shawl is doubled over, then the upper edge is folded over again. Long shawls and square shawls are worn in this manner. **3.** Traveling manteau of gray wool mousseline, with matching moiré banding, fringe, and soutache.

1   2   3

Toilettes by Mme Rossignon, rue de Provence. **1.** Toilette for young lady. Pink taffeta petticoat. Underdress of pink tarlatan with a double ruche separated by white and pink bias taffeta bands; overdress of white tarlatan, matching ruche. **2.** Pale green satin dress with velvet rouleaux. Court train of green velvet, trimmed with white lace. **3.** Underdress of quilted pink satin, trimmed with crystal buttons; overdress of pink velvet in a deeper shade, pink satin ruche.

1–3. Three ways to wear a net scarf. **4–9.** Coiffures by M. Croisat, rue Ménars.

2

1

3

5

4

1. Bodice with fichu. 2.
Sailor bodice. 3. Bodice
with vestee. 4. Tucked
mousseline bodice. 5.
Mousseline bodice with
bretelles. 6. Mousseline
bodice with simulated
corselet.

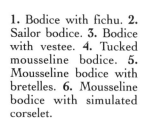

6

Parasols.

Toilettes by Mme Fladry, rue du Faubourg-Poissonnière. **1.** Costume for little girl of 4 to 6. **2.** Costume with Figaro fichu. **3.** Costume for little girl of 4 to 6. **4.** Costume for little girl of 6 to 8. **5.** At-home costume of violet wool. **6.** Costume for little girl of 3 to 5. **7.** Costume for girl of 10 to 12. **8.** Costume for girl of 11 to 13. **9.** Costume of black cashmere. **10.** Costume with Figaro fichu. **11–13.** Spring toilettes. **14.** Riding habit of Irish linen. **15.** Riding habit in vanilla wool. **16.** Riding habit of black wool.

1   2   3   4

11   12   13

5   6   7   8   9   10

14   15   16

Toilettes by Mme Fladry, rue du Faubourg-Poissonière. **1.** Dress of "Suez toast"-colored wool. Matching manteau trimmed with fringe. **2.** Gray faille dress with Indian shawl arranged as manteau. **3.** Evening dress in black-and-gold satin striped silk. Sortie de bal in white wool velours trimmed with three gold bands. **4.** Underdress of violet satin. Overdress in black faille, edged with a pleated ruffle. Black velvet manteau, trimmed in marten.

Autumn confections from Mme Fladry, rue du Faubourg-Poissonière. **1.** Albanian paletot. **2.** Elisabeth paletot. **3.** Albanian paletot (back view). **4.** Peri paletot. **5.** Margot paletot.

1

2

1–2. Sortie de théâtre by Mme Fladry, rue du Faubourg-Poissonière. 3–6. Toilettes by Mme Rossignon, rue de Provence. 3. Bertha with basque. 4. Décolleté bodice with basque. 5. Black net bodice. 6. Mousseline bertha.

3   4   5   6

1. Waterproof manteau. 2. Fitted jacket with basque. 3. Travel and rain manteau. 4. Black cashmere jacket and fanchon of white wool with violet ribbons (back view). 5. Black cashmere jacket and knitted fanchon in white wool. 6. Gray wool jacket and fanchon in white wool with violet ribbons (front). 7. Knitted pelerine with hood (back view). 8. Costume for young matron.

1   2   3

4   5   6   7   8

Winter pardessus from Mme Fladry, rue Richer. 1. Costume of poplin and silk armure. 2. Pardessus in wool velours. 3. Paletot in faille. 4. Paletot of black velvet. 5–6. Wool manteau (back and front). 7. Pardessus of lined cashmere.

Skaters. Models from Mme Maury, rue de la Michodière.

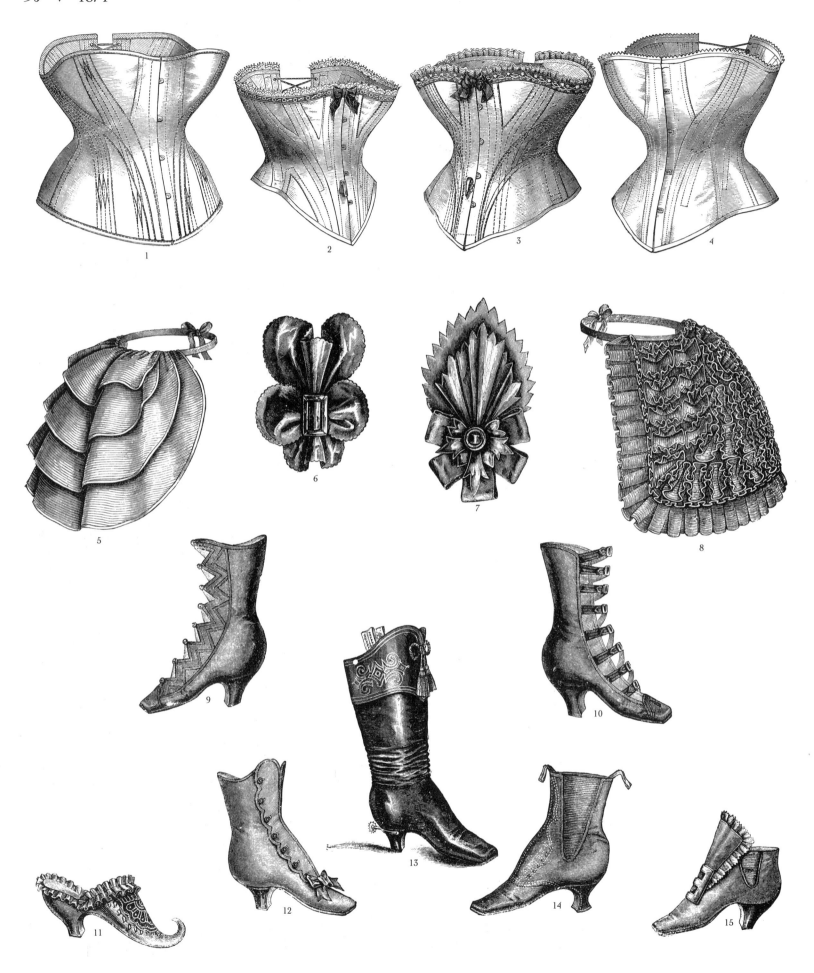

1. Reps corset. 2. Short corset. 3. English coutil corset. 4. Coutil corset. 5. Stiff gauze tournure. 6. Patent leather shoe bow. 7. Bow of morocco leather and ribbon. 8. Horsehair tournure. 9. Kid boot. 10. Open boot. 11. Slipper *à la poulaine*. 12. Buttoned demi-boot. 13. Riding boot. 14. Demi-boot. 15. Demi-bottine.

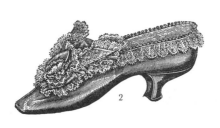

1

2

3

4   5   6   7   8

1. Bride's shoe bow. **2.** Bride's shoe. **3.** Bow for ball slipper. **4–8.** Toilettes by Mme Fladry, rue Richer. **4.** Bridal toilette in faille. **5.** Costume for little girl of 7 to 9. **6.** Satin bridal toilette. **7.** White silk bridal toilette. **8.** Town costume.

Winter chapeaux by Mme Aubert, rue Laffitte. 1. Dressy cap. 2. Brown velvet hat.
3. Hat with black velvet facing, front and back views. 4. Myrtle green velvet toque.
5. Black velvet hat. 6. Felt hat.

Toilettes by Mme Rossignon, rue de Provence.

1   2   3

1–6. Chapeaux by Mme Aubert, rue de la Victoire. ". . . the supreme law for the hat is to be ravishing.
A vague prescription, but hardly difficult, now that styles are so lovely." Mallarmé, *La Dernière Mode*.

7. Summer toilettes by Mme Fladry, rue Richer.

4

5

6

8

9

10

11

8–11. Toilettes by Mme Fladry, rue Richer. **8.** Black velvet jacket. **9.** Gray-blue wool casaque. **10.** Toilette of vicuna and faille. **11.** Toilette of black faille.

Ball and evening toilettes by Mme Fladry, rue Richer. **1.** Dress in pale lilac faille. **2.** Dress of white tulle. **3.** Dress of pink and garnet satin. **4.** Dress of silk gauze.

5. Dress of taffeta and tulle. **6.** Dress of faille and gauze. **7.** Dress of faille with lace flounces. **8.** Dress of bronze satin.

From Mme Massieu, rue Poissonière. Almée scarf of white net, with two rows of fluted white lace.

Evening toilette by Mme Fladry, rue Richer. The skirt and bodice are pink faille; a wide pleated flounce of white tulle is on the skirt. White tulle tunic trimmed with blonde lace and garlands of roses.

Summer toilettes by Mme Fladry, rue Richer.

Riding habits by Mme Bréant-Castel, rue du Quatre-Septembre. **1.** Dark gray-blue wool riding habit. **2.** Black wool riding habit. **3.** Costume of white and ecru batiste. **4.** Brown wool riding habit.

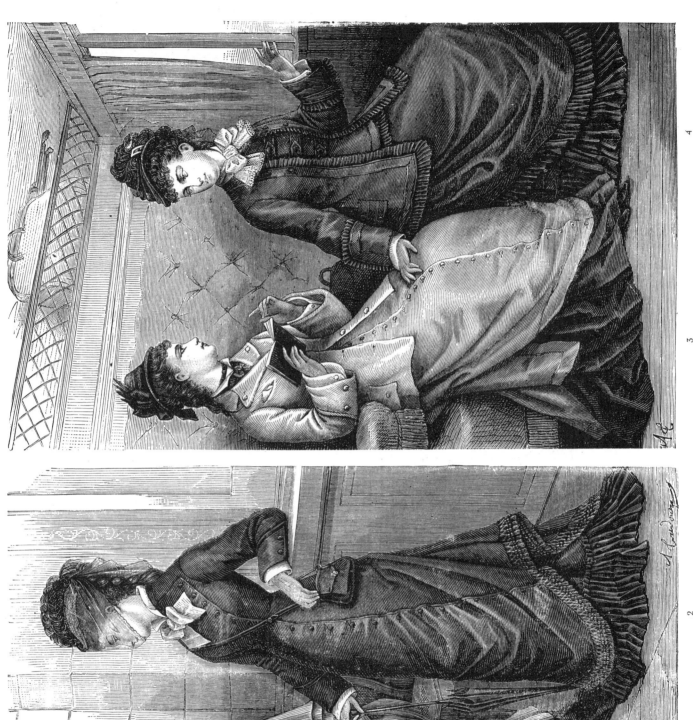

Travel toilettes by Mme Fladry, rue Richer. **1.** Manteau of striped waterproof fabric. **2.** Toilette in summer vicuna. **3.** Toilette of faille and cashmere. **4.** Toilette of summer armure and faille.

Lunch toilettes. Dresses from Mme Fladry, rue Richer; aprons from Mme Esther Massieu, rue Poissonière. 1. Toilette for an elderly lady. 2. Cashmere and velvet dress; muslin apron. 3. Girl's toilette. 4. Young lady's toilette. 5. Faille dress; batiste apron.

Ball toilettes by Mme Fladry, rue Richer. **1.** Dress of satin and crepe. **2.** Crepe toilette for young lady. **3.** Tarlatan dress. **4.** Dress of tulle and faille. **5.** Dress of faille

and silk gauze. **6.** Dress in tulle and poult-de-soie. **7.** Dress of silk gauze. **8.** Dress in satin and tulle.

Bathing and swimming costumes from Mmes Maury and Leriche, rue Vivienne.

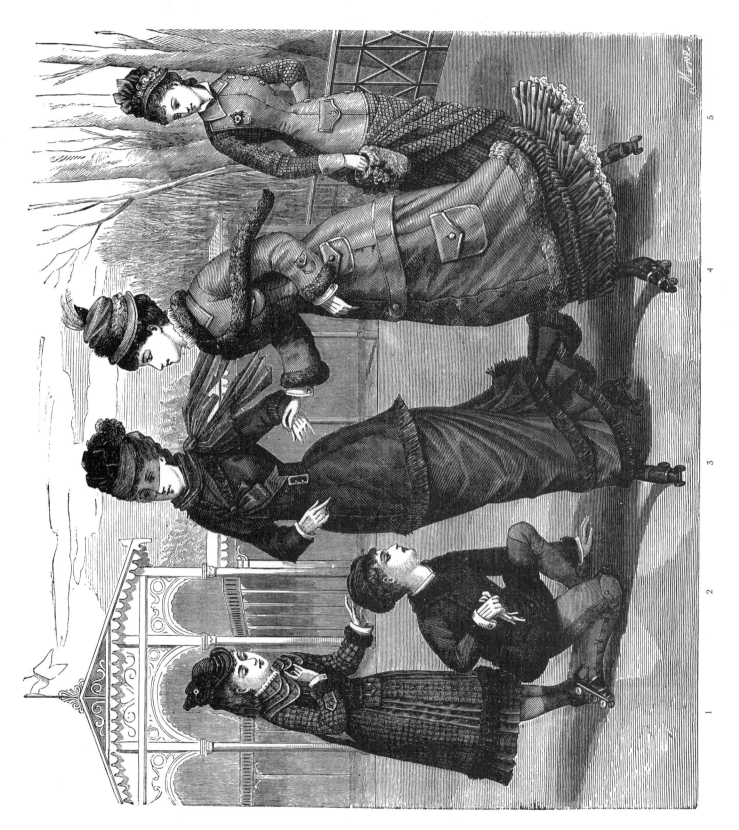

Skating toilettes by Mme Fladry, rue Richer. 1. Dress for girl of 9 to 11. 2. Costume for youth of 11 to 13. 3. Toilette of solid color Indian cashmere. 4. Vicuna toilette. 5. Tartan toilette.

From Mme Delaunay, rue Godot-de-Mauroy. **1–2.** Mourning hats. **3–4.** Mourning handkerchiefs. **5.** Crepe mourning bonnet. **6.** Mourning jewelry. **7.** Mourning hat in crepe. **8.** Mourning toilette in cashmere and crepe. **9.** Mourning toilette in cashmere. Widow's mourning lasted eighteen months; during the first six, only wool or crepe were worn, and the widow remained in seclusion. In the next six months jet jewelry and black lace were permitted, and some serious activities could be resumed. The last six months half-mourning colors (gray, white, and mauve) were worn and most social engagements permitted.

1. Summer boot. 2. Shoe. 3. Large umbrella. 4. Shoe. 5. Change purse. 6. Large umbrella. 7. Boot of kid and silk. 8. Shoe. 9. Travel hat worn five ways by Mme Deloffre, rue de L'Échiquier.

From Mme Bréant-Castel, rue du Quatre-Septembre. **1.** Suit for little boy of 5 to 7.
2. Dress of faille and patterned cashmere.

From Mme Coussinet (formerly Maison Fladry), rue Richer. **1.** Formal occasion toilette in velvet and brocade. **2.** Reception toilette in velvet and woven pattern cashmere.

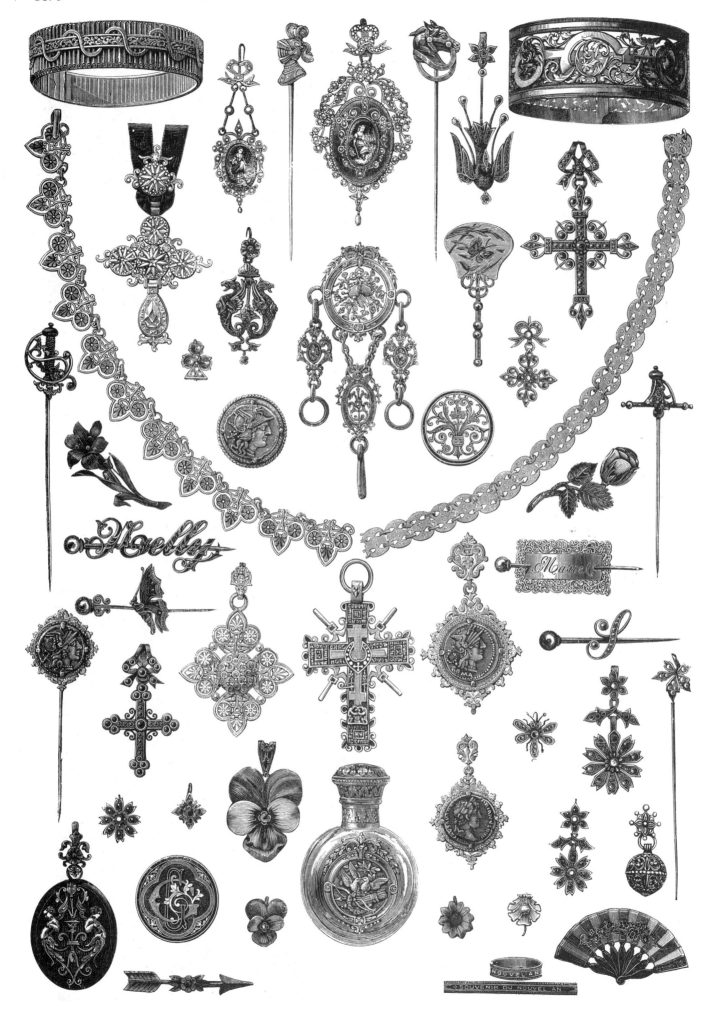

Artistic jewelry for New Year's gifts. Created by M. Marc Gueyton, place de la Madeleine.

1. Hat for the country. **2.** Fan and Parasols. **3.** Round hat. **4.** Coiffures for young ladies.

Ball toilettes by Mme Coussinet, rue Richer. **1.** Satin.
2. Satin and tulle. **3.** Tarlatan. **4.** Faille and tulle. **5.** Satin

with chenille latticework. **6.** Faille and crepeline. **7.** Faille
and brocade. **8.** Tulle and faille. **9.** Satin. **10.** Satin.

Winter pardessus by Mme Coussinet, rue Richer. **1.** Paletot for little boy of 6 to 8.
2. Dress for little girl of 3 to 5. **3.** Paletot for little girl of 6 to 8. **4.** Manteau of wide-
ribbed satin merveilleux. **5.** Town suit in plain and plaid satin with plaid satin man-

7 8 9 10 11 12

telet. **6.** Manteau of English wool. **7.** Manteau in satin à la reine. **8.** Paletot in béarnaise wool. **9.** Dress for little girl of 4 to 6. **10.** Cashmere suit. **11.** Manteau of wool bouclé. **12.** Visite with hood.

From Mme Coussinet, rue Richer. **1.** Dress in satin merveilleux. **2.** Toilette in surah. **3.** Velvet dress.

From Mme Coussinet, rue Richer. **1.** Young lady's suit. **2.** Dress of white batiste and blue satin damask merveilleux. **3.** White broderie anglaise percale dress, over plum surah underdress.

Mantelet of white mousseline from Mme Esther Massieu, rue Poissonière.

Three summer chapeaux by Mme Villedieu, Rue Sainte-Anne. **1.** Large round hat in white English straw, trimmed with bordeaux satin ribbon and a wreath of red roses. **2.** Italian straw trimmed with pale yellow satin ribbon and wild roses. **3.** White shiny straw trimmed with lace and roses with green leaves.

Winter chapeaux by Mme Deloffre, rue de l'Échiquier. **1.** Otter-brown beaver. The brim is covered in otter velvet and raised on the left side. Trim of two large matching feathers falling in back and ribbon striped in red, blue, green, and gold. A doe's foot with a gilded hoof is attached on the right side. **2.** Deep olive green velvet. The form is made of stiff net, covered in velvet. The hat is adorned with a border of olive and antique gold feathers. An aigrette, of the same feathers and heron feathers, trims the left side. Ties of olive satin ribbon. **3.** Deep olive green felt. Plush felt brim raised on the left side. A band of olive velvet encircles the crown, passes in front on the edge of the brim, is folded over on the right side and ends in a knot. A gilded metal pin and three pale bronze feathers with red tips adorn the hat. **4.** Otter felt. The brim is adorned with a feather border. A pleated triangle of moiré on the right side of the crown is held by a long gilded metal pin. A long ombré feather falls down the back. **5.** Soft black felt, with high crown. The plush brim is raised on the left side and trimmed with beaded lace. The trim consists of six feathers falling on the right side, and two leaf-shaped jet pins. **6.** Otter plush felt. Wide brim is trimmed with bows of otter satin and a bunch of plush roses and leaves.

Manteau fashioned from an uncut Indian shawl, front and back views. Model by
Mme de la Torchère, rue du Four-Saint-Germain.

1. Man's at-home suit. **2.** Men's suits from Grands
Magasins du Louvre. **3.** Man's wrapper and house
cap. **4.** Nainsook apron.

1   2

From Mme Coussinet, rue Richer. **1.** Dress of satin merveilleux and mousseline de
laine. **2.** Dress of cashmere and satin merveilleux.

Evening or dinner toilette.

Dinner toilette.

1–3. Three winter chapeaux by Mme Deloffre, rue de l'Échiquier. **4–8.** Winter toilettes by Mme Coussinet, rue Richer. **4.** Manteau in English wool. **5.** Woolen dress. **6.** Dress for girl of 8 to 10. **7.** Redingote with braid frogs. **8.** Cashmere dress.

1–5. From Mlles Hunsinger, rue de l'Échiquier. 1. Spring manteau for little girl of 4 to 6. 2. Dress for little boy of 15 months to 2 years. 3. Suit for little boy of 3 to 4. 4. Suit for little boy of 6 to 8. 5. Dress for girl of 11 to 13. 6. Mousseline dress. 7. Plaid wool dress with wool bodice. 8. Back view of wool dress.

1–8. From Mme Coussinet, rue Richer. 1. Scarf of striped crepe. 2. Dinner toilette. 3. Dinner toilette in Japanese crepe. 4. Ball toilette in taffeta and net with chenille dots. 5. Dinner toilette with velvet bodice (back). 6. Half-mourning toilette. 7. Evening toilette. 8. Dinner toilette with velvet bodice. 9. Printed wool

dress (back and front views).
10. Dress for little girl of 5 to 7.
11. Manteau of brocaded velvet.
12. Redingote for young lady of 14 to
16. **13–16.** Fans and costume jewelry
from M. Senet, rue du Quatre-
Septembre. **13.** Silk fan. **14.** Feather
fan. **15.** Costume jewelry. **16.** Lace
fan.

Ball toilettes by Mme Coussinet, rue Richer. **1.** Evening dress in lace and satin. **2.** Evening dress in crepe and faille. **3.** Ball gown in brocaded satin and plain ottoman. **4.** Ball gown in crepe. **5.** Ball toilette in solid

6   7   8   9   10   11

gauze and striped gauze. **6.** Dress for little girl of 4 to 6. **7.** Dress for
child of 3 to 5. **8.** Evening toilette in satin and velvet. **9.** Dress for child
of 2 to 3. **10.** Toilette for young lady. **11.** Dress for little girl of 7 to 9.

Winter pardessus by Mme Coussinet, rue Richer. **1.** Pardessus for little girl of 4 to 6. **2.** Manteau for child of 2 to 4. **3.** Woolen manteau.
4. Manteau of patterned wool. **5.** Manteau of striped wool and vel-

7   8   9   10   11

vet. **6.** Dress for little girl of 4 to 6. **7.** Manteau of velvet and brocade.
8. Manteau of patterned wool (back view). **9.** Manteau in sicilienne
and damask. **10.** Dress for girl of 13 to 15. **11.** Velvet pardessus.

1   2   3

From Mme Delaunay, rue Godot-de-Mauroy. **1–2.** Vicuna manteau (back and front views). **3.** Woolen dress.

From Mme Coussinet, rue Richer. **1.** Striped wool dress. **2.** Serge dress with pelerine. **3.** Crocheted scarf-mantilla. **4.** Sailor suit for little boy of 4 to 6. **5.** Dress in batavia sateen.

1. Mantelet of damask velvet. 2. Paletot of heavy vicuna.

1

2

1. Mantelet of damask velvet. 2. Paletot of heavy vicuna.

Bodices and jackets. **1.** Round bodice in deep red antique satin, open over a cream-colored tucked crepe de chine plastron; revers and cuffs of the same crepe de chine; rosette of cream satin ribbon. **2.** Figaro jacket of deep blue velvet with silk pompons; a pale blue surah vest completes the costume. **3.** Bodice of net and moss green velvet edged with silk braid embroidered with iridescent bronze beads; a cream-colored embroidered net chemisette with sleeves completes the costume. **4.** Lustrous bronze wool jacket lined in old gold silk; embroidery of brown and old gold braid, old gold vest with collar and belt of brown velvet. **5.** Mousseline bodice for young girl, pleated, trimmed with satin ribbon tabs and metal buckles, the sleeves forming a bouillonné toward the elbow and ending in a lace ruche; high, pleated collar.

1. Suit for little boy of 7 to 9. **2.** Wool dress. **3.** Mantelet in damask velvet.

1

2

3

1–2. Dress of patterned wool and black velvet with chenille trim (front and back view). **3.** Dress of brown wool trimmed with wool braid woven with gold, for little girl of 5 to 7. The top part of the skirt is covered by a cashmere scarf; sailor collar and cuffs are of brown velvet.

Winter chapeaux by Mlle Boitte, rue d'Alger. **1.** Round hat in black silk felt with a high crown, trimmed with black velvet and a long amazon feather. **2.** Round hat of bronze silk felt for young lady, trimmed with matching velvet, bronze feathers, and white swansdown. **3.** Bonnet of black silk felt, trimmed with plush roses and black velvet bonnet strings.

From Mme Coussinet, rue Richer. **1.** Large wool manteau (back view). **2.** Wool and plush suit.

Toilette of ecru surah.

1. Dress in solid and brocaded silk. The skirt is otter color, and the overdress has
an otter ground brocaded in maize. Collar and cuffs of brown velvet with a scarf of
maize surah. 2. Dress in black velvet and dark gray sicilienne. Velvet collar, cuffs,
and insertions on bodice. 3. Voile dress in cream color for young lady trimmed with
cream wool braid woven with gold.

Bathing costumes from Mlle de la Torchère, rue de Rennes. **1.** Bathing suit for little boy of 4 to 6. **2.** Bathing suit for young lady. **3.** Bathing suit with manteau for lady. **4.** Bathing suit for little girl of 8 to 10. **5.** Bathing suit with bathing cap.

1. Riding habit in wool. **2.** Riding habit in mohair.

Layette articles from Grands Magasins du Louvre.

Trousseau underwear from Grands Magasins du Louvre. **1.** Day chemise. **2.** Day chemise. **3.** Nightdress in colored percale. **4.** Nightdress. **5.** Matinée. **6.** Dressing sacque. **7.** Dressing sacque (back). **8.** Drawers. **9.** Matinée (front and back). **10.** Drawers.

Winter chapeaux by Mlle Boitte, rue d'Alger. **1.** Gray felt faced with gray velvet, trimmed with wide gray faille ribbons encircling gray ostrich plumes. **2.** Renaissance toque in bronze wool embroidered in brown silk. Brown plush diadem trimmed with two brown-and-white birds. **3.** Bonnet for visiting and wedding ceremonies. Black velvet embroidered with large jet medallions. Black lace brim, pink velvet roses, pink ostrich plumes.

From Mme Gradoz, rue de Provence. **1.** Striped flannel dress. **2.** Wool and faille dress.

1. Dinner dress in red satin trimmed with black Chantilly lace and embroidered with dark red beads. The back of the basque is adorned with a red velvet ribbon bow.
2. Evening manteau of peacock blue plush is lined in quilted silk to match. Trim consists of embroidery in peacock blue silk and gold thread and bands of white fur.

1   2

From Mme Coussinet, rue Richer. **1.** Dress in black velvet and lace. **2.** Dress in otter French faille with brown velvet trim.

Spring toilettes and pardessus by Mme Coussinet, rue Richer.
1. Striped moiré and bengaline dress. **2.** Moiré and lightweight wool
dress. **3.** Suit for little girl of 8 to 10. **4.** Cashmere dress. **5.** Dress for

6   7   8   9   10

little girl of 7 to 9. **6.** Mantelet in brocaded peau-de-soie. **7.** Spring
manteau in lightweight wool. **8.** Plush pardessus with feather trim.
9. Bengaline dress. **10.** Moiré and cashmere dress.

Ball toilettes by Mme Coussinet, rue Richer. **1.** Dress in silk armure. **2.** Dress in crepon. **3.** Net dress for young lady. **4.** Dress in faille and embroidered mousseline de soie. **5.** Ball toi-

lette for young lady (back). **6.** Net dress for young lady (back).
7. Embroidered net dress for young lady. **8.** Dress in plush and
lace. **9.** Dress of lemon faille. **10.** Dress in moiré and lace.

1. Sortie de bal by Mme Coussinet, rue Richer. 2. Evening and ball coiffures decorated with flowers. Models by M. Camille, rue du Quatre-Septembre.

1–4. Chapeaux by Mme Colombin, rue de la Tour-d'Auvergne. 1. Toque Henri II. 2. Buffalo Bill hat. 3. Bonnet with large brim in pale gray felt. 4. Small Persian toque in black astrakhan, for a young lady. 5. Jeweled hat pins by Mme Senet, rue du Quatre-Septembre. 6. Jeweled hairpins.

Simple toilettes for the race-track and morning visits.

From Mme Coussinet, rue Richer. **1.** Bodice with lapels and cravat. **2.** Bodice with lapels, collar, and cravat. **3.** Cheviot dress for summer. **4.** Travel coat.

Five summer chapeaux from Mlle Boitte, rue d'Alger. **1.** Flat hat in black lace, raised on one side, trimmed with an appliqué of jet beads, jonquil yellow velvet ribbon, and flowers. **2.** Bonnet of black rice straw, trimmed with black faille ribbons edged with a grenadine ribbon embroidered with gold paillettes. **3.** Bonnet of white and yellow straw, trimmed with yellow crepe de chine and white feathers. **4.** Hat made of bands of openwork straw in natural and otter. The large brim is trimmed with otter ribbons and poppies, crepe facing. **5.** Bonnet toque in black lace, edged with gold braid; clusters of lilac flowers.

1–5. Shoes by M. Wolff, rue du Vieux-Colombier. 1–2. Ball slippers, the first trimmed with velvet violets and the second with twisted strands of pearls. 3. House slipper of wool lined in flannel and trimmed with marabou. 4. Glacé kid shoe with six clasps. 5. Travel boot in black crocodile and red patent leather, laced to the top, English heel, 3 cm. high. 6. Leather belt. 7. Jet belt. 8. Jet jewelry from Maison Daguin, passage du Saumon. 9. Hairpins and hatpins from Maison Senet, rue du Quatre-Septembre. The tortoiseshell pins are inlaid with pearls or rhinestones; the antique silver or gilt ones are inlaid with stones. 10. Reticule.

Summer toilettes by Mme Coussinet, rue Richer. **1.** Princesse dress. **2.** Bodice of machine-made lace. **3.** Dress for young matron or young lady. **4.** Duster in mohair or taffeta. **5.** Dress for a lady of a certain age. **6.** Toilette for a young lady.

From Mmes Coussinet-Piret, rue Richer. **1.** Dress of striped silk. **2.** Batiste dress. **3.** Crepon dress. **4.** Dress in machine-made lace (back). **5.** Dress with polonaise. **6.** Front of lace dress. **7.** Dress for little girl of 5 to 7.

Ball toilettes by Mmes Coussinet-Piret, rue Richer. **1.** Toilette in glacé silk. **2.** Empire toilette. **3.** Ball dress for young lady. **4.** Dress of damask and mousseline de soie. **5.** Tulle dress for

6   7   8   9   10

young lady. **6.** Robe Louis XV. **7.** Cream silk dress embroidered in gold. **8.** Embroidered mousseline dress for young
lady. **9.** Empire ball gown. **10.** Louis XIV dress.

1. Six winter chapeaux by Mme Colombin, rue de la Tour-d'Auvergne.
2–4. From Mmes Coussinet-Piret, rue Richer. 2. Promenade toilette in wool, trimmed with astrakhan. 3. Promenade toilette with Valois cape. 4. Wool dress embellished with embroidery.

1–2. From Mme Gradoz, rue de Provence. 1. Dress and pardessus Henri II. 2. Costume with Russian tunic. 3. All-purpose umbrellas. 4. Sticks for umbrellas and parasols.

1

2

3

4

1   2   3   4

Pardessus for fall and winter from Mmes Coussinet-Piret, rue Richer.
1. Paletot-sac in wool and velvet. **2.** Tartan manteau. **3–4.** Fur-trimmed vicuna manteau (front and back). **5.** Tartan manteau, lined

5   6   7   8   9

and trimmed with fur. **6.** Manteau in heavy, patterned silk, lined and trimmed with fur. **7.** Wool paletot, trimmed with fur. **8.** Cape-collar in wool; fur trimming. **9.** Paletot in velvet and silk reps.

1–2. From Mlle Rimbot, rue de Richelieu. 1. Low-necked dress for little girl of 2 to 3. 2. Embroidered toile dress for little girl of 4 to 6. 3–7. Summer toilettes by Maison Joyeuse, rue du Colisée. 3. Batiste dress for young lady. 4. Taffeta dress. 5. Piqué dress with appliqués. 6. White wool dress. 7. Liberty silk dress. Back Views: 8. White wool dress. 9. Piqué dress. 10. Taffeta dress.

1–3. From Magasins du Louvre. **1.** Apron for little girl of 2 to 3. **2.** Apron for girl of 10 to 12. **3.** Dress for young lady of 15 to 17. **4–8.** Seaside toilettes. **4.** Dress of silk and muslin. **5.** Taffeta dress with mousseline de soie bodice. **6.** White cheviot dress. **7.** Suit for little boy of 3 to 4. **8.** Dress for little girl of 6 to 8.

1　　2　　3

4　　5　　6　　7　　8

1   2   3

From Maison Bresson-Chauvet: Gueyton, successeur, rue du Marché-Saint-Honoré. **1–2.** Tea gown (front and back). Seen from the front, it is made of lilac and straw-colored striped silk, from the back, of white wool. The neckline is edged with a wide band of cream guipure which forms a collar in back and edges the lilac velvet tablier, ending with a ruffle of lilac silk gauze which also borders the top of the tablier. **3.** Costume with bodice of plaid velvet. The skirt is of chestnut wool. The open velvet bodice is completed by a white surah chemisette with embroidered collar and cuffs.

From Mmes Coussinet-Piret, rue Richer. **1.** Moiré dinner toilette. **2.** Wool dress. **3.**
Dress with embroidered wool jacket. **4.** Velvet and plush dress. **5.** Bengaline dress.
6. Veloutine dress.

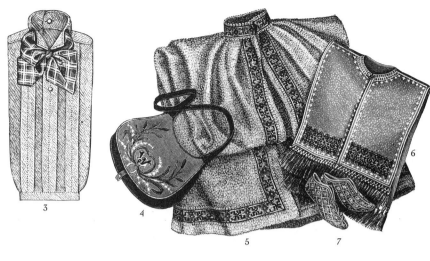

1 & 3. Shirtwaists in printed zephyr from Mlle de la Torchère, rue de Rennes. **2.** Spencer jacket for bicycling costume. **4.** Beach bag. **5.** Bathing coat. **6.** Neck towel for drying the hair. **7.** Bathing slippers. **8–9.** Models from Magasins du Louvre. **8.** Lawn-tennis costume in striped flannel. **9.** Lawn-tennis costume with revers on bodice.

From Magasins du Louvre. **1.** Boating costume. **2.** Bicycling costume with jersey bodice. **3.** Hiking costume.

Ball toilettes by Mmes Coussinet-Piret, rue Richer. **1.** Louis XIV toilette for middle-aged lady. **2.** Ball gown with pearl garniture for young lady. **3.** Velvet gown embroidered with pearls. **4.** Brocaded

satin gown with floral decoration. **5.** Mousseline de soie gown for young lady. **6.** Printed silk gown. **7.** Satin gown with feather trim. **8.** Satin gown with ruches. **9.** Changeable moiré gown.

From Mmes Coussinet-Piret, rue Richer. 1. Cape with fur neckpiece; toque. 2. Paletot decorated with wool braid; felt hat. 3. Morning suit with short paletot; felt hat. 4. Long paletot trimmed with fur; felt toque. 5. Large talma with appliqués and fur trim; plush bonnet for a lady of a certain age. 6. Dress of wool and embossed velvet.

From Mmes Coussinet-Piret, rue Richer. **1.** Striped wool dress trimmed with white wool. **2.** Jacket trimmed with braid. **3.** Silk mantelet. **4.** Dress for spring and travel.

From Mmes Coussinet-Piret, rue Richer. **1.** Coat for rain or travel. **2.** Duster. **3.** Piqué dress and jacket. **4.** Cream mohair dress with sleeveless jacket and green-and-blue plaid blouse. **5.** Dress with Empire jacket. **6.** Sailor dress for young lady. **7.** Dress with quarter-master jacket for little girl of 6 to 7. **8.** Dress with Louis XV jacket-bodice. **9.** Black mohair dress. **10.** Lawn dress.

J. CHAPUIS

1–2. Spring chapeaux by Mlle Boitte, rue d'Alger. 3–12. From Mmes Coussinet-Piret, rue Richer. 3. Dress with tab-shaped basques. 4. Wool dress with bead embroidery. 5. Dress with lace epaulettes. 6. Dress decorated with bead embroidery. 7. Jacket with revers. 8. Dress with

jacket. **9.** Elegant cape adorned with lace. **10.** Silk dress with pleated gauze bodice. **11.** Promenade or traveling dress. **12.** Cape with hood.

13–14. From Magasins du Louvre. **13.** Dress for little girl of 10 to 11. **14.** Dress for little girl of 9 to 10.

1   2   3

1–3. Fancy dress costumes from Mme Gradoz, rue de Provence. **1.** Columbine. **2.** Domino in satin. **3.** Aluminum.

4–18. Toilette accessories. **4.** Fan with wood sticks, painted bronze; mount is black net and verdigris silk. **5.** Fan with sticks of violet wood, decorated with paillettes. Mount of myrtle green silk with paillettes and insertions of black net. **6.** Lorgnette chain of red moiré ribbon with gold braid, amethysts, and pearls. **7.** Large rectangular belt buckle in gilt-bronze. **8.** Small button hook of gilt brass. **9.** Narrow olive green velvet belt, with antique silver and enamel ornaments, decorated with turquoises. **10–11.** Combs in blond shell in various sizes. **12.** Neck ruche of leaves of lilac silk and cream lace. **13.** Ivory gauze scarf woven with brightly colored flowers. **14.** Sortie de bal lined in quilted white moiré. Yoke with a Medici collar, covered with white silk and iridescent bead embroidery; the collar is faced with white Tibetan goat. **15.** A sable boa decorated in the back with two tails, ending in front with two crossed heads. **16.** Otter hat with a high crown and a band of marten on the brim. **17.** Dark beaver toque with a flat crown and narrow brim. **18.** Small chinchilla muff, trimmed with a head and two paws, and a tail on one side.

19–21. Toilettes for theater or formal occasions. From Mmes Coussinet-Piret, rue Richer. **19.** Gown of pale blue silk. The hem of the skirt is lightly embroidered with pearls. The square bodice is open in front, over a pale blue net blouse embroidered with pearls. The front of the jacket is trimmed with solid revers; the bodice is completed by bouffant sleeves trimmed with pleated ruffles, and by a pearl-embroidered Medici belt. **20.** Velvet gown consisting of a skirt with a small train, a pointed bodice, and short puffed sleeves. A cream silk gauze fichu edged with guipure is placed around the neckline, attached at the shoulders and knotted in front. **21.** Bodice in ivory crepe-chiffon over ivory taffeta; the blouse, lightly gathered at the bottom, is arranged in front and back in tiny horizontal and vertical tucks; between the tucks are insertions of Valenciennes. A plastron of pleated crepe-chiffon with four rows of shirred Valenciennes is attached to the front of the blouse. The tight collar is orange velvet. The belt is cream satin ribbon closed in back with a rosette.

From Mmes Coussinet-Piret, rue Richer.
1. Seaside suit in piqué. **2.** Foulard dress
trimmed with velvet ribbons. **3.** Seaside suit
for little girl of 7 to 8. **4.** Bathing suit with
bolero. **5.** Bathing suit for little girl of 6 to 7.
6. Bathing costume with washable braid
trim.

1   2   3   4   5   6

7. Serge bathing suit. 8. Suit with bathrobe. 9. Bathing suit in striped flannel. 10. Seaside costume with jacket. 11. Taffeta dress. 12. Scottish batiste dress with lace yoke.

Summer costumes from Mme Lacombe, rue du Faubourg-Saint-Honoré.

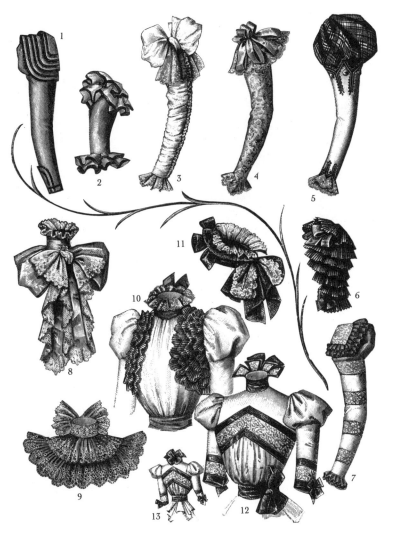

1–13. Group of sleeves and neckwear from Mmes Coussinet-Piret, rue Richer. **1.** Sleeve in covert-cloth or wool, trimmed with braid. **2.** Elbow-length sleeve of silk with shirred ruffles edged with velvet ribbon. **3.** Shirred sleeve in lightweight silk or wool. An embroidered ruffle at the shoulder is topped by a large bouffant bow. **4.** Lace over colored silk ending in two points at the wrist. **5.** Sleeve in wool and plaid silk trimmed with passementerie and a lace ruffle. **6.** Short sleeve composed entirely of pleated ruffles. **7.** Sleeve for etamine dresses; trim of lace insertions over colored silk ribbon, square epaulette of insertions and ribbon. **8.** The upper part of this garniture is made in black silk embroidered with pearls, while the bands and the rear bow are made of embroidered gauze. **9.** Neckwear trim of colored silk ribbon and cream lace; the tight ribbon collar encircles lace fraise; a large silk bow in front. **10.** This jacket-bolero serves to complete a blouse-bodice, trimmed with a tight collar and belt of silk. **11.** This garniture in cerise silk forms a large bow in front and a smaller one in back. **12–13.** Bodice trimmed with velvet ribbons and insertions. A black pleated belt encircles the waist and ends in a bow on the side. Square tabs of lace edged with velvet ribbon are attached to the tight collar. **14.** Group of trimmed skirts from Mlles de la Torchère et Sauveur, rue du Cherche-Midi.

Hunt meeting. Ladies' toilettes from Mmes Coussinet-Piret, rue Richer. Men's hunting suits from La Belle Jardinière. **1.** Autumn toilette. **2.** Hunting suit. **3.** Autumn toilette. **4.** Hunting suit. **5–6.** Headgear for hunting. **5.** Cap **6.** Fedora.

3   4

1. Men's toilet articles. 2. Town suit. 3. Bridegroom's suit from La Belle Jardinière. 4. At-home suit.

Nightdresses and undergarments trimmed with embroidery and ribbons. **1.** Corset trimmed with insertions. **2.** Underbodice. **3–4.** Combing jackets. **5–11.** From Magasins du Louvre. **5.** Two petticoats. **6.** Pale blue wool wrapper. **7.** Combing jacket. **8.** Matinée. **9.** Lingerie. **10.** Black patent leather shoes. **11.** Black silk stockings.

1

2

3

8

9

From Mmes Coussinet-Piret, rue Richer. **1.** Velvet promenade costume adorned with wide bands of fur. **2.** Ermine trimmed dress in tobacco-colored covert-cloth. Stitched wool bands form a large motif in front and encircle the skirt. Similar appliqués trim the open jacket with ermine revers. Yellow surah waist. The black silk felt hat is trimmed with gold silk and ostrich feathers. **3.** Dress with double skirt in sable-colored wool trimmed with bands of astrakhan and black chenille embroidery. **4.** Blue velvet dress trimmed with gold soutache. **5.** Silver gray cashmere and reddish brown velvet. Simulated yoke of guipure. **6.** Otter fur jacket with revers, Medici collar, and cuffs of chinchilla. **7.** Bolero jacket trimmed with black braid completes a toilette of red wool with a black silk waist. **8–9.** From Mme Colombin, rue de la Tour-d'Auvergne. **8.** Lady's toque in black velvet. Four ostrich plumes are held by a velvet chou and a strass buckle. **9.** Hat for young lady in tobacco-colored felt with brim edged in a lighter shade. Feathers trimmed with iridescent paillettes on both sides, large bow in front. **10.** Toilette for concerts, visiting, etc., in steel gray bengaline with a black velvet yoke ending in a Mary Stuart collar and framed by a fan-shaped border embroidered with paillettes.

Touring

From Mlle Louise Piret, rue Richer. **1.** Suit with fitted jacket. **2.** Travel outfit with jacket. **3.** Travel dress with bolero. **4.** Dress trimmed with bands of stitching and cape. **5.** Travel hat from Magasins du Louvre.

At the
Racetrack

From Ayme et Cie., boul. de la
Madeleine. **1.** Batiste toilette.
2. Dress with pleated bodice and
corselet. **3.** Organdy dress.
4. Toilette in printed foulard.
5. Toilette with unmatched bodice.
6. Elegant chapeau from Magasins
du Louvre.

Madame and dear reader,

We have received so many requests from our honorable gentlemen's clientele to open a department of tailored suits for ladies, that we could not but take account of such a legitimate and flattering desire, and . . . we are assuredly able to compete with the most skillful tailors in Paris and the great capitals.

We are now in a position, Madame, to furnish you with irreproachable tailored suits in the latest fashion, cut in magnificent materials, not the lightweight fabrics in general use which lack body and do not answer the requirements of the tailored suit.

To prepare ourselves for a happy introduction, we have not hesitated to establish a price of 95 francs for a custom-made suit, and for 69 fr. 50 a superb jacket completely lined in silk. We show here several of our models and we submit them without reservation for your highest approval, in the belief that before obtaining an order it is necessary above all to show proof of style and taste. *HIGH-LIFE TAILOR*

Visiting

Oh! my dear beauty, that delicious Nella outfit!—And you, dear Madame, what a ravishing Adrienne suit! Unnecessary, I am sure, to ask you the address of the magician?—Unnecessary, in effect, since there is but one.—High-Life Tailor. What style, what fabrics, what superb inspirations, what sublime creations!—And their staggering tailored suit at 95 francs, what a lovely introduction! . . . —And their silk-lined jackets at 69 fr. 50, what a challenge to the haute couture! Listen, chère belle; 112, rue de Richelieu. *All Right!*

At the Chrysanthemum Exhibition

This flower festival having become a glorification of feminine fashion, it was our duty to sketch several of these divine costumes which are provoking general admiration and praising to the skies the fast becoming famous name of High-Life Tailor. We reproduce here only a part of his work: only at his establishment can it be contemplated in its inexhaustible variety and ideal perfection. How the master couturier would be delighted if he were able to savor the praises that his suit at 95 francs inspired in his admirers! And the gentlemen . . . They feel the same about the luxury and taste of their raglan pardessus, at 69 fr. 50, which allows them to parade, without feeling inferior, in front of such queens of beauty.

We wished to present, in honor of our readers, some of the ravishing models which are causing tout Paris to run to the exhibition of feminine costumes, 112, rue de Richelieu, at the Boulevard. One cannot help but feel sincere admiration before these exquisite clothes, and above all the tailored suits at 95 francs, regal gift from High-Life Tailor, to the most select of the elegant world.

The great tailor couturier is willing to send his Illustrated Catalogue, a sumptuous museum of costume, but, to his great regret, he cannot accept orders from the provinces, the presence of his clients being indispensable to fit as he intends, all the de luxe or daytime garments that leave his establishment.

Portrait of Baroness de M. . . . wearing an elegant tailored suit made to order at the price of 95 francs by the High-Life Tailor, where at this moment the spring collection consists of no less than one hundred different models of these ravishing costumes.

L. KOWALSKY

Spring and summer chapeaux by Mme Colombin, rue de la Tour-d'Auvergne. **1.** Toque in lawn and woven otter straw, trimmed on the side with a bunch of black currants and tea roses, surmounted by an aigrette of lawn. **2.** Sand-colored toque. The pleated brim is embroidered with pretty straw motifs on net; the bottom, in velvety leaves, is raised on the side by two turquoise plumes, the underpart of the hat is adorned with sand and turquoise taffeta, ending in a streamer. **3.** Round hat, edged with roses of various shades, is veiled by jet-sprinkled lace; a bunch of roses with a round pearl pin raises the side of the brim slightly. **4.** Hat of ombréd violet straw. The brim is trimmed with antique guipure, two bands of black velvet, and a bunch of shaded roses and thistles.

1. Automobile coat. 2. Hunting suit
for young matron. 3. Excursion
suit for girl of 10 to 12. 4. Man's
hunting suit.

From Maison Finet, rue du Temple. **1.** Automobile costume in green and white wool trimmed with stitched bands. White flannel shirtwaist, starched collar worn with cravat. **2.** Duster of Tussor silk, with stitched pleats, closed with five mother-of-pearl buttons, tight cuffs. **3.** Bicycling costume. Dark gray homespun with stitched homespun piping. The lined skirt is divided to form trousers. Black-and-white striped silk trim, white flannel chemisette with starched collar, and cravat.

Formal toilettes by Mlle Louise Piret, rue Richer. 1. Elegant dress for elderly lady. 2. Toilette for young matron. 3. Nurse's cape. 4. Baby pelisse. 5. Suit for 9- to 10-year-old boy. 6. Man's suit. 7. Elegant dress for 14- to 15-year-old girl.

Toilettes for morning and formal occasions by Mlle Louise Piret, rue Richer.
1. Toilette for young lady or young matron. 2. Dress for elderly lady. 3. Toilette of
Liberty silk. 4. Toilette for middle-aged lady. 5. Toilette for young matron.

12

14

1   2   3   4   5

1–13. From Mlle Louise Piret, rue Richer. **1.** Dress for a girl of 10 to 12. **2.** Wool toilette with redingote. **3.** Velvet toilette for young lady. **4.** Elegant visiting toilette. **5.** Wool dress with new skirt. **6.** Empire ball toilette. **7.** Ball gown in yellow panné velvet for a middle-aged lady. **8.** Ball toilette for a young lady. **9.** Ball toilette for a

middle-aged lady. **10.** Princesse style ball toilette. **11.** Blouse for a lady of a certain age. **12.** Back views of town toilettes. **13.** Back views of ball toilettes. **14–15.** From Maison Camille, rue du Quatre-Septembre. **14.** Ball coiffure for young matron. **15.** Ball coiffure for young lady.

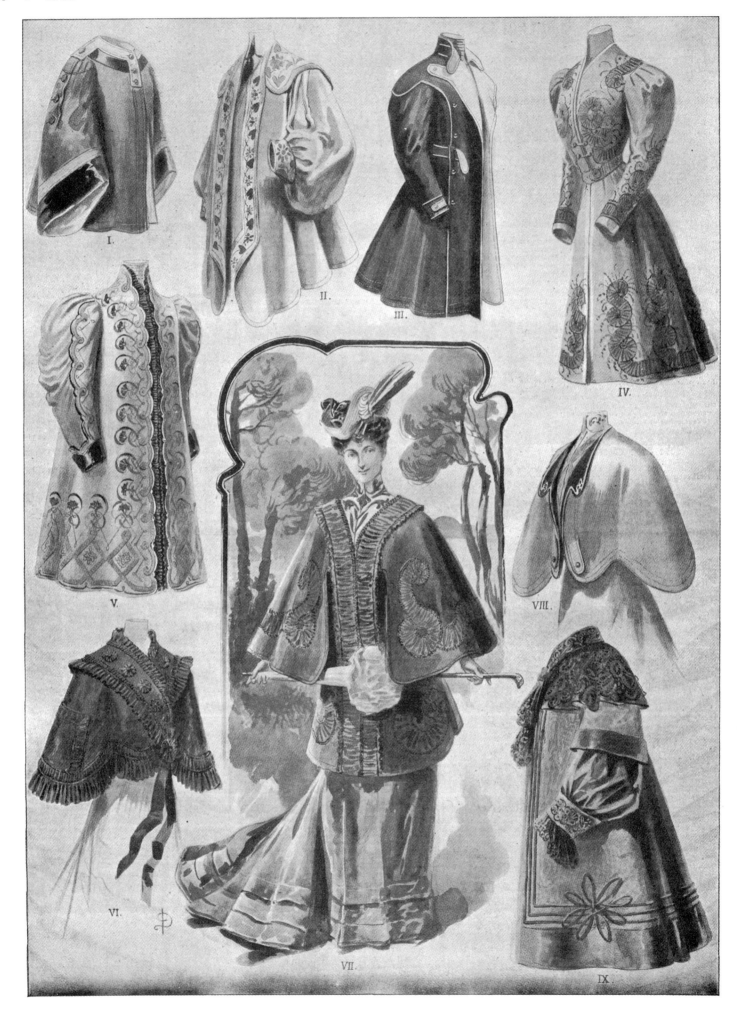

Mid-season coats.

Waists and skirts.

1. Town toilette by Doucet, worn by Mlle Milo d'Arcyle in *Le Maître des Forges*. Pink mousseline de soie, pleated skirt trimmed with three rows of lace insertions with narrow Valenciennes edging. Bodice with lace yoke framed in embroidered pink taffeta. Wide belt trimmed with painted floral white porcelain buttons. 2. Morning toilette by Doucet, worn by Mlle Gilda Darthy in *Le Maître des Forges*. Pale blue soft velvet, full skirt and draped bodice with ecru lace yoke, trimmed with velvet piping. Elbow-length sleeves edged with écru lace ruffles. 3. Formal occasion toilette for a middle-aged lady. Model by Mlle Goèry, rue Littré.

1. Tailored suit by Redfern. Light gray wool tone-on-tone plaid, pleats stitched on the hips, widening toward the hem to create the necessary fullness. The jacket is tailored with stitched pleats held at the shoulder by fancy buttons; the tiny revers are fixed with the help of matching buttons. The jacket is open over a vest of white cloth with edging of gold embroidery and black-and-white striped silk. 2. Chapeau for young matron by Maison Virot. Toque of draped ruby velvet raised on the left side by a gray ostrich plume held by a bow of silver ribbon. 3. Tailored suit for walking or visiting by High-Life Tailor. The green cloth skirt is encircled by four rows of piping ending at center front inverted pleat. The jacket with basque and embroidered revers, opens over a white cloth vest with embroidered trim.

1. Sylphide costume for young lady. 2. Ball toilette for young matron.
3. Dinner toilette. 4. Ball or dinner toilette for middle-aged lady.
5. Elegant toilette for 8- to 10-year-old girl. 6. Elegant cloth paletot.
7. Wool suit for young lady. 8. Promenade toilette. 9. Russian peasant cos-

11

9

6 7 8

15 16 17

tume for young lady or young matron. **10.** Mary Stuart headdress.
11. Salambô headdress for *dîner de têtes*. Back Views: **12.** Toilette for middle-aged lady. **13.** Dinner toilette. **14.** Ball toilette for young matron.
15. Promenade toilette. **16.** Elegant paletot. **17.** Wool suit for young lady.

1   2

11   12

13   14   15

3

4

5

6

8   9   10

From Mlle Louise Piret, rue Richer. **1.** Suit for boy of 8 to 10. **2.** Dress for girl of 11 to 13. **3.** Dress for little girl of 4 to 6. **4.** Spring dress for young lady. **5.** Suit for town or travel. **6.** Spring Empire paletot. **7.** Summer dress for young matron. **8.** Simple dress for elderly lady. **9.** Spring toilette for young lady. **10.** Tailored suit for girl of 15 to 17. Back Views: **11.** Spring dress for young lady. **12.** Town or travel suit. **13.** Simple dress for elderly lady. **14.** Spring toilette for young lady. **15.** Summer dress for young matron.

7

Autumn toilettes by Drecoll. **1.** Wool dress. **2.** Dress for young lady. **3.** Mid-season costume. **4.** Empire dress.

5   6   7   8

5. Striped velvet dress. **6.** Wool dress with embroidered trim.
7. Dress with hooded bolero. **8.** Dress for middle-aged lady.

Toilettes and chapeaux from Magasins du Printemps.
1. Winter suit with little straight paletot. **2.** Walking dress.

5   6   7

3. Toilette for formal occasions. **4.** Visiting toilette. **5.** Tailored suit. **6.** Toilette in taffeta. **7.** Costume trimmed with braid.

From Chèruit, formerly Raudnitz et Cie., place Vendôme. **1.** Costume with long basque of réséda green satin-finish wool with passementerie and fancy buttons. Vest, high collar, and cuffs of pale yellow cloth. **2.** Spring costume with redingote, for visiting and going out. Pale gray wool skirt and old rose redingote. Guipure plastron. Soutache trim and old rose velvet piping. **3.** Dress trimmed with pleats and piping. **4.** Tailored costume for a young lady. **5.** Back view of three toilettes at left.

From Mme Blanche Limousin, rue La Fayette. 1. Sequined tulle bolero for special-occasion dress. 2–6. From Mme Blanche Limousin, rue La Fayette. 2. Ball toilette. 3. Empire-style ball toilette. 4. Dinner or formal-occasion toilette. Back Views: 5. Ball toilette. 6. Empire-style ball toilette. 7. Dinner toilette.

1. Chapeau for a young matron. Lustrous bronze straw, round crown wreathed with roses and leaves. A large feather shaded from brown to pink falls in back over the hair. 2. Watering-place toilette. Liberty silk with black coin dots. The bodice has a wide belt and a shawl collar with silk revers ending in crossed tabs; the cream lawn vestee is trimmed with Irish lace. Elbow-length sleeves with lace insets and Irish lace ruffles at elbow. 3. Toilette for the races. Supple taffeta with full skirt, trimmed at the hem with wide piping. The bodice has Japanese sleeves and is open over a vestee with high collar in mousseline trimmed with lace. 4. Resort dress. Blue-and-white striped wool, trimmed with passementerie and soutache in blue silk. The bodice is lightly

1

2   3

4   5

bloused and embroidered with a blue silk anchor. **5.** Dress for the seaside. Serge dress trimmed with silk piping framed by soutache. The white serge plastron is trimmed with silk piping. Shawl collar with silk cravat. Belt with antique silver buckle. **6.** Yachting costume in ecru tussor, white silk collar with embroidered anchors. **7.** Casino toilette with demi-Empire skirt, in crepe de chine meteore, trimmed with Venetian guipure. **8.** Afternoon toilette in fancy striped foulard has a demi-Empire skirt with guipure insertions, shirred at the waist and mounted on a wide belt. Bodice of guipure over a point d'esprit waist, velvet ribbon trim. **9.** Elegant chapeau adorned with marabou.

6

7   8

1. Automobile coat with matching cap. This unlined coat is made of double-faced checked wool; mother-of-pearl buttons. 2. Bicycling suit. Gray covert-cloth with collar, lapels, and trim of red velvet. Taffeta-lined jacket, horn buttons. 3. Riding habit with divided skirt of black wool for riding astride. 4. Automobile hat and veil. The gray felt hat has a striped leather band and feathers. The veil, which covers the entire head, is held on by means of an elastic, the front edged with a channel threaded with a silk ribbon which fastens under the chin and hides the joining of the mica mask. 5. Suit for sport or travel. Plaid wool with bands of stitching above hem of skirt with inverted pleats, stitching on jacket. 6. Back views of figures on this page. 7. Man's suit. 8. Man's one-button suit. 9. Man's overcoat.

1. White flannel tennis costume, consisting of a skirt made of six groups of four pleats each, and a pleated waist with stiff collar. Blue silk belt and cravat and white cap. **2.** Automobile paletot of gray bias-check English wool, piped in a darker shade. Large buttons. **3.** Bolero jacket. **4.** Riding habit. **5.** Travel or automobile coat.

1

2

3

4

5

1

2

1. Afternoon dress by Paquin in emerald green Liberty satin. The bodice has a lace plastron and is adorned with Pompadour embroidery. 2. Manteau by Drecoll. Champagne wool, draped on the shoulders, is lined with emerald green Liberty silk. The neck is edged with a tiny collar holding the scarf with champagne silk tassels at the ends. Dress is of Parma wool with lace plastron trimmed with passementerie buttons.

1

2

1. Afternoon dress by Martial and Armand, in aubergine Liberty satin. The skirt, ending in a draped belt, is trimmed with an insertion of appliqué embroidery. The draped bodice is made with a plastron framed by an embroidered garniture ending in front in knotted fringe. **2.** Dress for a young lady by Chèruit, in old rose Liberty crepon, held at the waist by a narrow sash in a deeper rose, ending in silver tassels. The bodice has a round décolletage, edged with lace.

1. Fur-trimmed dress. **2.** Walking suit. **3.** Elegant town costume by Mlle Louise Piret, rue Richer.

1. Visiting dress. **2.** Mid-season manteau.

1. New coiffures by Maison Heng, rue Bergère. 2. Chapeaux for young matron and young lady by Mme Colombin, rue de la Tour-d'Auvergne. 3–8. From Mlle Louise Piret, rue Richer. 3. Princesse dress with paletot of soutache-embroidered net. 4. Summer dress for elderly lady. 5. Foulard dress.

13   14   15

2

6   7   8

6. Tussor toilette. 7. Piqué dress for
young lady. 8. Elegant batiste toilette. Back Views: 9. Dress for
elderly lady. 10. Foulard dress.
11. Other view of princesse dress.
12. Paletot of soutache-embroidered net. 13. Tussor toilette.
14. Piqué dress for young lady.
15. Elegant batiste toilette.

1

11

12   13

3   4   5   6

1–2. From Mme Colombin, rue de la Tour-d'Auvergne. **1.** Winter hat for young lady or young matron. **2.** Headdress for evening. **3.** Elegant winter manteau. **4.** Town dress. **5.** Wool paletot trimmed with fur. **6.** Velvet toilette. **7.** Manteau for

7   8   9   10

16   17

girl of 13 to 15. **8.** Dress with tunic. **9.** Long winter paletot. **10.** Fur paletot. Back
Views: **11.** Elegant winter manteau. **12.** Town dress. **13.** Fur-trimmed paletot.
14. Velvet toilette. **15.** Dress with tunic. **16.** Long winter paletot. **17.** Fur paletot.

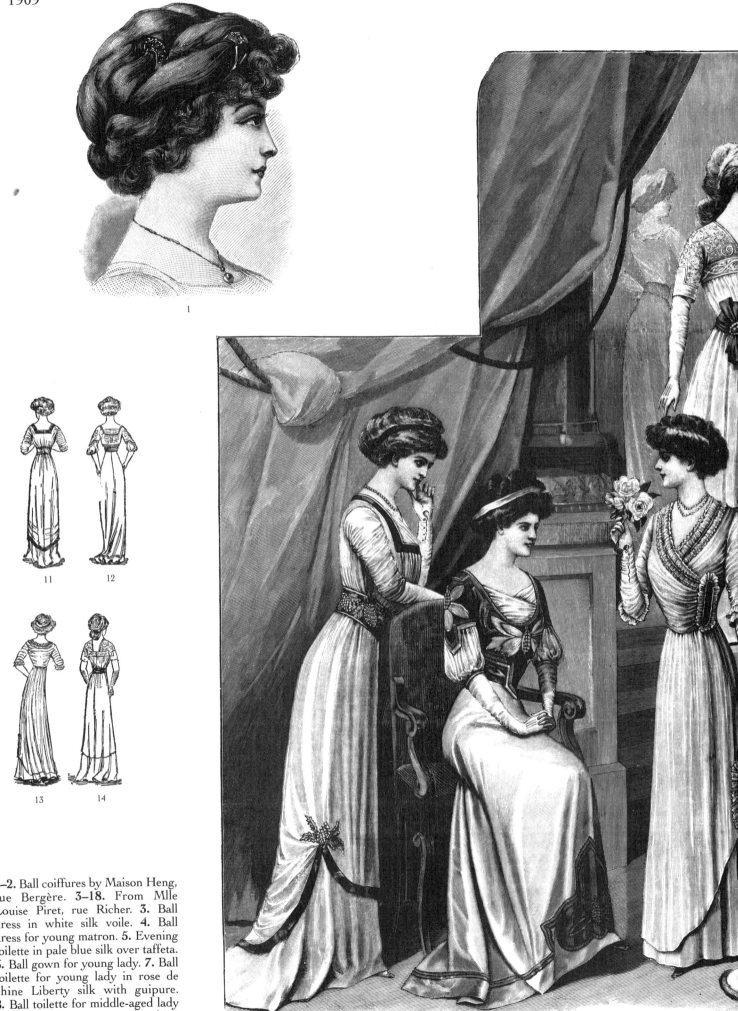

1

11 12

13 14

3 4 5 6

1–2. Ball coiffures by Maison Heng, rue Bergère. 3–18. From Mlle Louise Piret, rue Richer. 3. Ball dress in white silk voile. 4. Ball dress for young matron. 5. Evening toilette in pale blue silk over taffeta. 6. Ball gown for young lady. 7. Ball toilette for young lady in rose de chine Liberty silk with guipure. 8. Ball toilette for middle-aged lady in willow green crepe de chine edged with sable. 9. Princesse-style

dinner or ball gown for a lady of a certain age in amethyst velvet. **10.** Ball toilette in apricot mousseline de soie. Back Views: **11.** Ball gown in silk voile. **12.** Ball toilette for young matron. **13.** Evening toilette. **14.** Ball gown for young lady. **15.** Liberty silk for young lady. **16.** Ball gown for middle-aged lady. **17.** Dinner or ball gown for a lady of a certain age. **18.** Ball toilette in mousseline de soie.

From Mlles Sauveur de la Torchère, rue du Cherche-Midi. **1.** Summer chapeau of coarse straw, raised in back, large printed foulard bow, wreath of daisies. **2.** Ottoman paletot in lustrous bronze, with tabbed details on hips and collar. **3.** Foulard dress in mauve printed with darker circles. White openwork batiste guimpe with button trim, Liberty revers matching the dress, lace collar and cuffs. **4.** Striped batiste dress in blue and white, pleated lawn plastron, embroidered collar, cuffs, and

1

2

3

4

insertion on skirt. **5.** Simple toile dress in Delft blue, draped black satin belt. **6.** Casino dress in mauve shantung, batiste guimpe ending in a collarette, large guipure collar and matching cuffs, draped silk sash to match the dress. **7.** Resort toilette in pink foulard with deeper polka dots, bands of soutache trim bodice and skirt, lawn yoke and pleated cuffs at elbow, draped silk sash. **8.** Garden or travel chapeau, large cloche in natural straw edged with brown velvet, dotted cream foulard trim, knotted on one side.

5

8

6

7

Jean the next day.

1. Simple tailored suit in two-tone brown-striped cheviot. Revers, collar, and cuffs faced in black silk edged in white. Brown leather belt. **2.** Wool dress for young matron. Putty-colored, trimmed with rich embroidery in Nattier blue. The surplice bodice is open over a tucked white net guimpe, framed by a draped fichu in Nattier blue silk. **3.** Pink shantung dress with a round skirt for young lady. Wide yoke pleated to form two wide revers in back; the skirt hem has a wide border of chestnut silk cashmere. Embroidered lawn collar and undersleeves. **4.** Blue silk afternoon dress. The skirt has a small train encircled with a wide black satin band. The bodice is covered by an embroidered mousseline de soie blouson, edged in black satin, the top open over a high-collared yoke of ecru net framed by a little guimpe embroidered in gold and steel. **5.** Walking suit in cypress green wool, round skirt crossing in front. Long jacket with shawl collar.

MONDAN.

Aunt Susan the next day

1. Tailored suit by Bechoff-David. **2.** Walking suit by Antoine and Hubert. **3.** Mourning dress for middle-aged lady from Maison Poilane. **4.** Town toilette in red-and-gray checked foulard by Margaine-Lacroix. **5.** Visiting toilette in old rose mousseline de soie.

1–2. Summer chapeaux for girls. 1. Fine natural straw with a wide, draped almond green ribbon. 2. Large brimmed hat in Italian straw, white lace edging, red cherries with leaves. 3–9. Summer dresses for children and girls of 3 to 14. 3. Dress for 4- to 6-year-old. Fine white wool, draped silk sash. Collar, cuffs, and trim of green silk with blue dots. 4. Dress for 7- to 9-year-old. Light gray serge; bloused bodice trimmed with buckles and silk buttons. White lace yoke framed by soutache of same color as dress. 5. Dress for little girl of 5 to 7. Cream cashmere; sailor collar, cravat, and cuffs of pale blue silk. Guipure yoke and sleeves. 6. Dress for girl of 12 to 14. Unlined blue voile, embroidered batiste collar and cuffs. Fabric belt with buckle, jabot of batiste and Valenciennes lace. 7. Dress for child of 2 to 4. Red wool with a fabric belt. Long-waisted, bloused bodice appliquéd with soutache at the side closing. Embroidered collar and cuffs. 8. Dress for girl of 9 to 11. Brick red fine serge, trimmed with matching panné velvet and cream-colored guipure.

1–6. Dresses for girls and young ladies. **1.** Royal blue velvet tunic dress for young lady. **2.** Blue reps with soutache trim for girl of 14 to 16. **3.** Dress for big girl of white wool piped in antique blue silk. **4.** Suit with lace plastron for girl. **5.** Brown silk cashmere dress with matching silk trim for young lady. **6.** Striped wool dress for young lady. **7–8.** Summer hats for girls 6 to 11 from Mme Colombin, rue de la Tour-d'Auvergne. **7.** Dutch bonnet in light and dark blue straw, adorned on each side with points of pleated straw. Faced in black velvet. **8.** Beret in blue and red glossy taffeta. The large crown is draped over a wire frame and trimmed with a band of roses.

Jean the first night

1. Evening toilette. Steel blue Liberty silk, garniture of cream-colored guipure edging the tunic and rising to the hip on one side. The opposite side has a guipure panel which descends from the V-necked bodice. 2. Theater coiffure. Center part, sides combed back or rolled to form a twist; the hair is waved softly in front. Pailletted net ornament with a spray of white feathers. 3. Ball dress for young lady. Pale blue pleated charmeuse skirt and dotted net tunic edged with lace. Charmeuse bodice with V-neck décolletage and lace bertha. Pale blue ribbon sash. 4. Ball toilette. White charmeuse enriched with green pailletted braid. Surplice bodice; the front is decorated with a small rounded corselet of emerald silk. The sleeves are edged with beaded fringe. 5. Formal dress for lady of a certain age. Black net over royal blue Liberty satin, with a small train. Silk belt decorated with cabochons. 6. Toilette for young matron. Lemon yellow Liberty silk with a tunic of black embroidered net, open in front. The top of the bodice is draped mousseline de soie, held by a jeweled

brooch. The short sleeves are edged with skunk. The top of the skirt is edged with white beads. **7.** Ball gown. Chinese pink charmeuse dress with a pleated mousseline de soie tunic in the same shade. The tunic is edged with embroidery, placed below a band of sable, which also edges the décolletage. **8.** Evening toilette for young lady. White silk, the hem banded with white fur or swansdown; the skirt has panniers, one of which is bordered with white mousseline de soie roses. The sleeves and left side of the surplice bodice are edged with fur, the right side is trimmed with pink roses. **9.** Ball coiffure. Waved hair parted in the center, swept to the back and arranged in little knots. A double row of beads is attached to a ribbon which encircles the back of the head, with a jeweled pin holding a white aigrette. **10.** Evening gown. Yellow charmeuse trimmed with skunk and black silk. The décolleté bodice and the hem are embellished with embroidered paillettes. The sleeves end in beaded fringe, the tunic has a black silk tassel.

1–8. Afternoon dresses for winter.
1. Dress in fancy-weave wool. 2. Dress
of velvet and taffeta. 3. Dress embellished with lace. 4. Dress for young
lady. 5. Dress with draped panniers.
6. Dress embellished with braid.
7. Dress with tunic skirt. 8. Dress
trimmed with fur. 9–10. Chapeaux by
Mme Colombin. 9. Chapeau of
stretched velvet. 10. Chapeau of plush.

Winter fashions. **1–2.** From Mme Colombin, rue de la Tour-d'Auvergne. **1.** Velvet chapeau. **2.** Large velvet beret. **3.** Winter paletot of brown herringbone with collar and cuffs of brown velvet. **4.** Velvet manteau. Black velvet lined in antique blue satin, black passementerie embellishes the collar and cuffs. **5.** Town costume. Mouse gray velvet skirt. Matching silk paletot with kimono sleeves. Gray satin facing on lapels. **6.** Suit in solid and striped wool velvet. Gray-and-white striped skirt, gray jacket, with gray fox collar, cuffs, and band at hem. **7.** Suit in taupe cor-

duroy with four-gore skirt, wrapped in front. Astrakhan collar, braid trim at hem. **8.** Suit of fine rust serge. Fabric button trim on skirt and sleeves. **9.** Manteau in gray ratiné with khaki-colored shawl collar and cuffs. **10.** Fur overcoat. Can be made of real fur or imitation fur in silk plush or velvet, with collar and cuffs of real fur. The matching muff is thickly padded and lined in satin. Back Views. **11.** Velvet manteau. **12.** Serge suit. **13.** Striped velvet. **14.** Fur overcoat. **15.** Manteau. **16.** Town costume.

Winter costumes for girls and boys. **1.** Overcoat for big girl, in ratiné or velvet; if made in velvet, the pockets and collar could be satin or fur. **2.** Fur-edged skating costume in Russian green or otter brown velvet. **3.** Paletot for a boy, with velvet collar and suit to match. **4.** Skating outfit consisting of a bright green velvet skirt and a jacket with basque in a tricot-like material. **5.** Outfit for little girl consisting of a long, unfitted jacket trimmed with plaid and a matching suspender skirt. **6.** Boy's white jersey for sports. In color, it would be suitable for school.

For Winter Sports

1. Jacket for sport or travel. Wide-wale violet wool velvet, cerise duvetyn collar and buttons. **2.** Sports jacket and cap. Leaf green wool suede; raglan sleeves, covered buttons, wide cuffs, large pockets. The cap is edged with a band of chamois-colored wool. **3.** English wool tweed suit with raglan sleeves and flap pockets. **4.** White ribbed velvet skating suit and cap. To be more practical, it may be made in dark gray, brown, or green. The skirt wraps in front and has a low half-belt in back. The collar is hidden under a fox neckpiece to match the trim on the cap. **5.** Jacket of teddy bear fabric, with raglan sleeves, wide self belt, and patch pockets. Felt hat with teddy bear fabric brim facing. **6.** Kimono sleeve paletot for sport or travel; rows of stitching trim collar, sleeve seams, and wrists. **7.** Knitted jacket for sports to wear with a skirt which can be velvet or wool. Knitted stocking cap and scarf.

New Fashions in Lingerie

1. Princesse combination in batiste with insertions of lace and embroidery. **2.** Corset of white silk batiste is boned halfway, the bottom is laced; ribbon and lace trim. **3–5.** Chemise, drawers, and corset cover of batiste embellished with embroidered insertions with ribbon and edged with Valenciennes; the drawers are made with groups of tiny pleats. **6.** Batiste nightdress with little pleats, mounted on a yoke with an openwork border through which a ribbon is threaded; short sleeves cut in one piece with the yoke. **7.** Combing cape of batiste trimmed with large scallops, closing with a large mother-of-pearl button. **8.** Boudoir cap of batiste, edged with a narrow band of lace.

Fashions for the Bridal Party

1. Bride's toilette of cream satin, matching brocade, and embroidered net. The draped satin skirt ends in a brocade train and is open in front, caught by orange blossoms, over a net underskirt. The veil is attached on both sides with roses. **2.** Toilette for bridesmaid. Blue silk voile trimmed with geranium pink satin. Collar may be of Irish, Venetian, or Renaissance lace. **3.** Bride's dress of white satin and mousseline de soie. The trim consists of garlands of orange blossoms which also wreathe the tulle veil. **4.** Toilette for member of wedding party. Black lace over bright green satin. Bodice is draped fichu-style to reveal a glimpse of cream net partly hidden by a band of gold lace. This dress would also be very pretty with a white, salmon, or apricot ground. **5.** Bride's headdress and Medici collar. The off-the-face veil of tulle is shirred twice, each row hidden by a garland of orange blossoms. Medici collar of Renaissance embroidery. **6–9.** Back views.

New Fashions for
the Afternoon

1. Chapeau for young lady, by Mme Colombin, rue de la Tour-d'Auvergne. 2–9. From Mmes Balmain Soeurs, rue de la Chaussée-d'Antin. 2. Afternoon dress of charmeuse with draped tunic. Kimono-sleeved bodice opens over a plastron of white moiré.

White moiré sailor collar with lace trim. 3. Dress with bolero bodice. 4. Dress of surah trimmed with gathered pleats. 5. Toilette of soft silk. Back Views: 6. Dress with bolero bodice. 7. Dress with gathered pleat trim. 8. Afternoon dress with draped tunic. 9. Soft silk toilette.

Visiting

From Mlles Sauveur, rue du Cherche-Midi. **1–2.** Suit of cypress green velvet, covered buttons and belt. Fur collar and cuffs. **3–4.** Visiting dress with skirt of tobacco satin and kimono-sleeved bodice of embroidered white silk. Corselet with bretelles of black velvet. **5–6.** Dress for young matron of black silk and peacock blue silk voile. The kimono-sleeved voile bodice crosses in front, as does the black, sleeveless blouson. Venetian lace guimpe and Medici collar. **7–8.** Suit for young lady in smooth chamois wool, trimmed simply with fox. A very wide stitched waistband connects the jacket and basque.

Evening and Ball Gowns

aunt susan the first night

1–2. Theater toilette of brocaded and solid silk, with a small train and gathered tunic, open in front. Rope of pearls knotted in front serves as sash. 3–4. Ball gown for young matron. Pailletted tulle skirt over black mousseline de soie. Bodice has short kimono sleeves concealed by long scarves ending in tassels, joined at the waist in back. Model by Balmain Soeurs, rue de la Chaussée d'Antin. 5. Ball coiffure with jeweled diadem and aigrette, by Maison Heng, rue Bergère. 6–7. Toilette for young matron. Pale pink taffeta and white lace, the skirt made with draped panniers which fall over a lace tunic. The bodice is a lace kimono with a taffeta corselet edged with a fluted ruffle, held by a garland of roses. 8–9. Evening toilette. Ivory silk brocade skirt hemmed with skunk. Lace tunic edged with skunk, open in front to reveal a mousseline fichu.

For Evening

1. Evening dress in bronze chiffon velvet and beige brocaded silk.
2. Evening coat of berry red moiré, embellished with antique gold embroidery. Lining of brocaded mousseline de soie, silk cord tied below knees. 3. Coiffure for a lady of a certain age, by Maison Heng, rue Bergère. 4. Evening coat of Empire green satin trimmed with a wide fox collar and band at the hem. The sleeves, black satin with fur cuffs, emerge from openings embellished with embroidered braid. 5. Theater dress of supple material with draped panniers. Vestee is white mousseline de soie. Medici collar and net undersleeves embroidered in gold.

Resort Wear

From Mlles Sauveur, rue du Cherche-Midi. **1.** Morning dress. Beige toile with soutache-trimmed coral toile collar and cuffs. Bloused bodice, fagoted shoulder seams and hem band. **2.** Casino dress of cream silk, cream-and-green plaid silk trim. Organdy vestee with Medici collar. **3.** Duster with cape. Can be made in alpaca, tussor, or waterproof silk. Silk plaid facing and hat. **4.** Walking dress. Green-and-blue striped taffeta with a little blue silk jacket. The skirt is mounted on a grosgrain corselet with bretelles. The bodice is open over a white organdy vestee with Medici collar. **5.** Afternoon dress. White voile trimmed with black-and-white striped voile. The narrow skirt is encircled by striped ruffles cut on the bias. Striped bodice and vest, with Medici collar of white organdy.

The Latest Novelties for Summer

1. Walking dress. Navy blue serge skirt, green serge jacket trimmed with blue piping. Kimono sleeves with double ruffles of lace. Lawn vestee edged in lace with Medici collar. 2. Town dress. Skirt of striped silk, solid silk tunic. Kimono bodice open in front over a plastron. Satin collar, long sleeves trimmed with a row of buttons. 3. Dress for elderly lady. Plum silk over an underdress of the same color. Slightly raised waistline. Long-sleeved bodice is made with fichu composed of two bands of fabric crossed in front, joined with a tab embroidered with matching tassels; the guimpe has a high collar of cream net. 4. Dress for young lady. Long sleeves, round décolletage with button trim, over a pleated gilet with sailor collar. 5. Visiting dress. Solid silk with brocaded silk bolero ending in solid basque. The bolero crosses and closes with one button, showing a batiste chemisette.

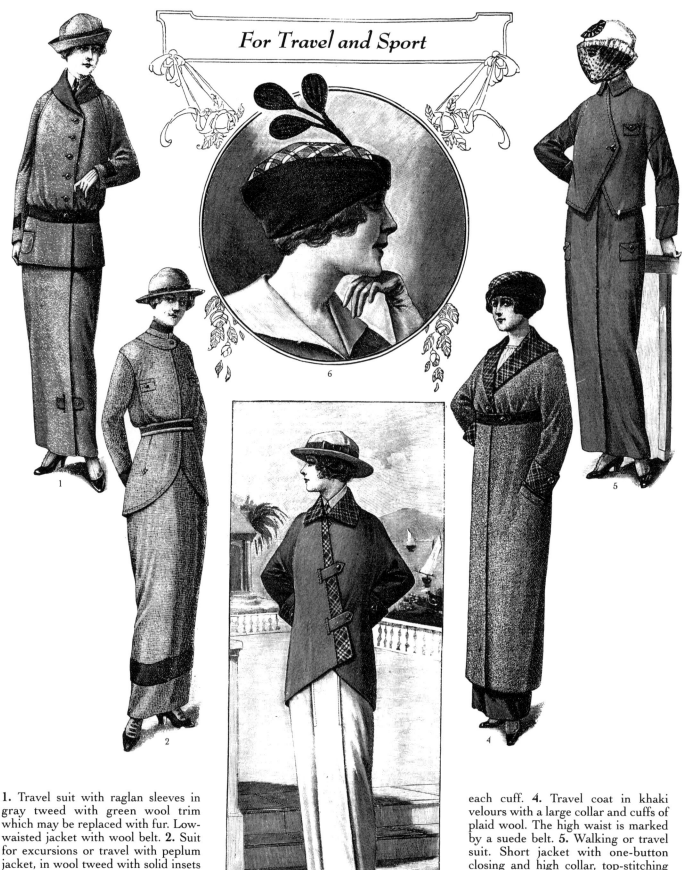

For Travel and Sport

1

2

3

4

5

6

1. Travel suit with raglan sleeves in gray tweed with green wool trim which may be replaced with fur. Low-waisted jacket with wool belt. **2.** Suit for excursions or travel with peplum jacket, in wool tweed with solid insets at neck, belt, and hem. **3.** Resort suit with white cheviot skirt and bouclé jacket in blue, green, or red, trimmed with plaid wool. Kimono sleeves, diagonal closing with two tabs, tab also on each cuff. **4.** Travel coat in khaki velours with a large collar and cuffs of plaid wool. The high waist is marked by a suede belt. **5.** Walking or travel suit. Short jacket with one-button closing and high collar, top-stitching details on jacket. **6.** Walking hat. Taffeta brim and plaid taffeta crown with fantasy trim. Model by Mme Colombin, rue de la Tour-d'Auvergne.

For Travel and Sport

1. Gabardine suit. Skirt has pleats in front and back to give sufficient fullness while retaining the narrow look which is so modern. Jacket closes with tortoiseshell buttons. 2–3. Automobile coat and hat. May be made in tussor, voile, or wool. Our model is in white ratiné trimmed with khaki ratiné and khaki-and-white striped silk. Matching hat in solid and striped khaki, fullness gathered under the striped band stiffened with muslin. 4–5. Raincoat with raglan sleeves and shawl collar. Half-belt in front, concealed placket closing. 6. Sports suit with short skirt. Green wool skirt, green-and-brown bias plaid jacket. Shawl collar, cuffs, and belt match skirt; horn buttons.

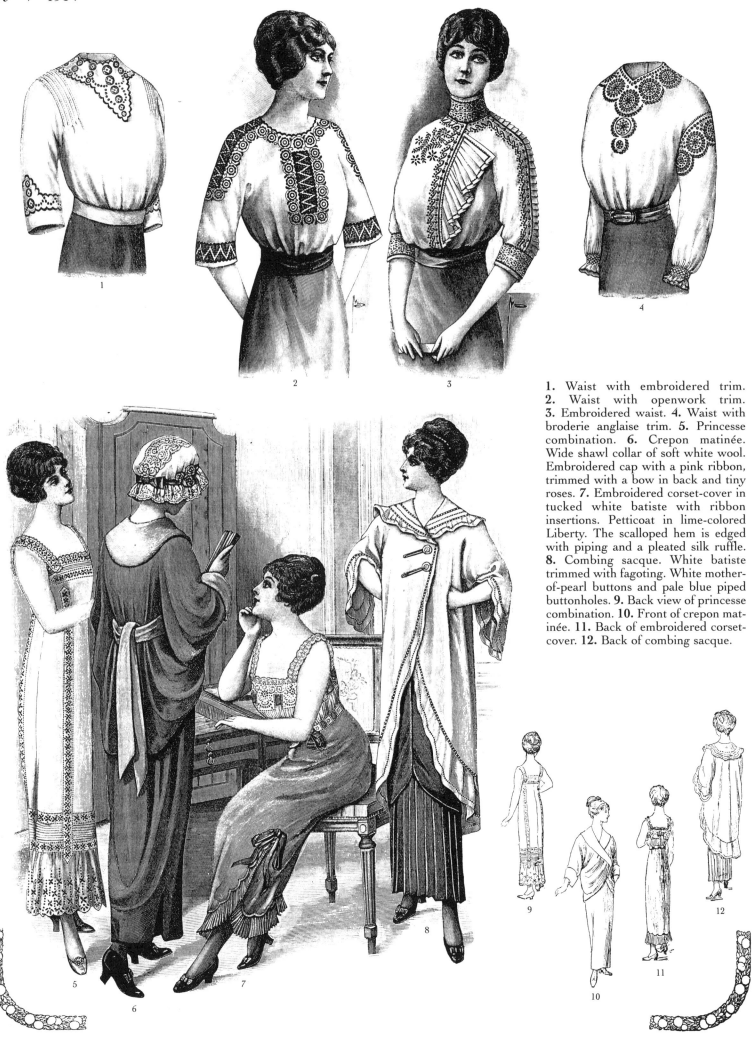

1. Waist with embroidered trim.
2. Waist with openwork trim.
3. Embroidered waist. 4. Waist with broderie anglaise trim. 5. Princesse combination. 6. Crepon matinée. Wide shawl collar of soft white wool. Embroidered cap with a pink ribbon, trimmed with a bow in back and tiny roses. 7. Embroidered corset-cover in tucked white batiste with ribbon insertions. Petticoat in lime-colored Liberty. The scalloped hem is edged with piping and a pleated silk ruffle. 8. Combing sacque. White batiste trimmed with fagoting. White mother-of-pearl buttons and pale blue piped buttonholes. 9. Back view of princesse combination. 10. Front of crepon matinée. 11. Back of embroidered corset-cover. 12. Back of combing sacque.

Fashions for the Young Bride

1. Toilette for civil ceremony by Mlles Sauveur, rue du Cherche-Midi. Antique blue charmeuse, trimmed with lace. Kimono bodice is arranged in pleats ending on the shoulder. Collar and cuffs of lace. **2.** Afternoon toilette with Medici collar. **3.** Simple dress. Cabbage green cashmere trimmed with lighter green satin and zig-zag soutache. **4.** Evening toilette. Pale pink crepe de chine with bodice and overtunic of maline. **5.** Bride's toilette. Made of charmeuse, the edges of the tunic and the bodice are outlined with a wide insertion of maline. Net guimpe with high collar lined in mousseline de soie. The waist is encircled by a draped charmeuse belt.

1. Bride's toilette. **2.** Bridesmaid's toilette.